ENCOURAGEMENT
from me to you

ENCOURAGEMENT
from me to you

Melinda Doljac

TATE PUBLISHING
AND ENTERPRISES, LLC

Published by Tate Publishing & Enterprises, LLC
127 E. Trade Center Terrace | Mustang, Oklahoma 73064 USA
1.888.361.9473 | www.tatepublishing.com

Tate Publishing is committed to excellence in the publishing industry. The company reflects the philosophy established by the founders, based on Psalm 68:11,
"The Lord gave the word and great was the company of those who published it."

Book design copyright © 2015 by Tate Publishing, LLC. All rights reserved.
Cover design by Niño Carlo Suico
Interior design by Gram Telen

Published in the United States of America

ISBN: 978-1-68028-420-1
1. Religion / Christian Life / Devotional
2. Religion / Christian Life / Inspirational
14.12.09

Contents

1

Life

The whole discipline of life is to enter into a close relationship with Jesus Christ. We receive His blessings and know His Word, but do we really know Him? Once we get intimate with Jesus, we are never lonely, we can always pour out our concerns upon Him. He is always with us. People will see in us the strong, calming nature that our Lord gives to those who are intimate with Him.

Live your life like you have a race to run—like there is a prize at the end of your life. There is, to be able to spend eternity with Jesus in a brand new body just like the one He has now, in heaven with Him and all your loved ones who love the Lord. He wants us to live a pure life, a holy life in Him. Run that race and keep your eyes upon the prize!

Jesus tells us that we must turn our back on our old life… and have a new life in Him. We all are a part of the Great Commission! Not just pastors. All of us must turn our back on the old man of the world and follow God. The Great Commission is a command from Jesus for you and me.

We do not have to worry about achieving or finding the meaning of life. It has come to us in the person of Jesus Christ.

If you search for the Lord with all of your heart, you will find Him.

Seek the Lord; repent of your sins and humble yourselves unto the Lord. We each have business to do with God.

The Lord loves us so much that He gave us a choice on how to live our lives. He gave us the free will to live for Him, the Creator of all things. Or to live to please ourselves, usually in the pleasures of the world, which Satan is in control of. We have a choice to make, the Lord or Satan.

We all have a life to lead. The Lord gave some of us a spouse for companionship, and He gave us a gift of children. Never take your spouse or your children over the Lord. Never love your spouse or your children more than you love Jesus. They cannot promise you eternal life. The love you have for Jesus should totally outweigh the love you have for your family or worldly possessions.

You say that you cannot stop talking about your children or your grandchildren? You must do the same if not more talking about Christ. Jesus is to be your number one passion.

Fall in love with Jesus, and you will not want to stop talking about Him. Let Him be your passion, the love of your life. He loved you enough to die for you.

The Lord has called us to be His messengers, to proclaim to men the way of life. He calls all of us to be His messengers to be a witness for Him, at home, the gym, at the store and yes, even at church. He is calling you to be His messenger, learn His Word and ask Him where He wants to use you to glorify Him.

We should live up to our light, but if that light is itself darkness, what a mistake our whole lives will be!

"It is better to hear the rebuke of the wise, than for a man to hear the song of fools" (Eccles. 7:5).

We have to be careful. We are not to be seen with the wrong types of people and in the wrong worldly places; it will bring our testimony down. Someone is always watching for you to slip up!

We are to live our lives according to the Word of God. When we read the Word, we must live what we read. We must be "doers of the Word" not hearers only. This will not give any glory to the Lord.

This is a wonderful life the Lord gave to us. Is the Lord proud of how you are living your life? If not, the Lord wants you to be a new person in Christ Jesus, to throw away the old sinful man and to be a new man in Christ Jesus.

The moment we take our eyes off Jesus is a calling card for Satan to come into your life; do not let that happen to you!

When you do not understand what is going on in your life, put your trust in God and believe there is nothing too hard for God.

The Lord gives and the Lord takes away. Blessed is the Lord!

Life is not about you, and it is not about me. Life is about placing the Creator of all things, the God of heaven and earth, the God that can give you a great inheritance with Him forever—we are to give Him our all.

We are to love the Lord more than we love ourselves. We are to live our lives according to His training manual, the Bible, and not what man decides is correct. Man can always lead the Lord's children astray.

Expect the Lord to move in your life and He will move!

In this day and age, everyone thinks that they are so wise in their living for themselves and in their acceptance of the world's views. This is what the Lord tells us through Paul:

"Let no one deceive himself. If anyone among you seems to be wise in this age, let him become a fool that he may become wise. For the wisdom of this world is foolishness with God. For it is written. He catches the wise in their own craftiness" (1 Cor. 3:18–19).

Yes, that sums it up; it is time to be humble before your God, to turn your back on worldliness, and to live for Him and not the sinful world. We are not to put our trust in the world, only in God.

We are to pour out all of our hope and trust into the Lord. Put Him in control, we must stop trying to run our own life. Give it to Jesus to run and enjoy the ride!

Take a step back. Is the Lord proud of how you are living your life? If not, the Lord wants you to be a new person in Christ Jesus, to throw away the old sinful man and to be a reflection of Him.

The big question is: do we want to be believers in the Lord, or just simple followers? Remember the parable of the talents. The servant who doubled the talents was granted so much more, and the one who buried the talent in the ground was banished from the Lord.

"And cast the unprofitable servant into the outer darkness. There will be weeping and gnashing of teeth" (Matt. 25:30).

Serve the Lord; do not be like the unprofitable servant. What a horrible fate.

Jesus says: "And the King will answer and say to them, Assuredly, I say to you, in as much as you did it to one of the least of these My brethren, you did it to Me" (Matt. 25:40).

Let people see Christ in you. Let your children see Christ in you that would be the best gift you could ever give to them!

Yes, we are to search for the Lord with all of our hearts and for a close relationship with Jesus. If we search for Him, if we have a hunger and a passion for Him, He will find us.

Christ is the missing piece of the puzzle of life that you have sought for so long. Satan would have you fight against this truth till you die.

Life is not about us...it is all about Christ.

Life is about becoming a faithful servant. It takes an intimate relationship with God. Study His Word, live what you read, and serve Him. He will open doors in your life for you to serve Him.

Be careful who you let enter your inner circle. Bad company corrupts good character!

Who is your best friend? Who do you run to in times of trouble? Let it be Jesus, only Jesus.

If we indeed live for the Lord, it is written: "Eye has not seen, nor ear heard, nor have entered into the heart of man the things which God has prepared for those who love Him" (1 Cor. 2:9).

Jesus does not want part of us; He wants all of us. Give your life to Him. He gave His for you, and He promises you eternal life forever with Him.

Jesus tells us not to look back on our past lives, just keep on following Him. You will be greatly blessed.

Each of us shall give account of himself to God. So please live a pure and righteous life.

People that follow Jesus are not to use their lives on earth for their own pleasure; they should spend their lives serving God and others.

We are all on a journey in life. We have a choice as to which road to go down. Jesus is calling.

Life is not about the here and now. It is about eternity. We are to serve the risen Lord. What will He say as we stand before His throne? We should have a hunger to hear those precious words from the Lord. "Well done, My faithful servant, you served Me well."

"That you may love the LORD your God, that you may obey His voice and that you may cling to Him. For He is your life and the length of your days" (Deut. 30:20a).

Stop patting yourself on the back because of everything you are doing in your life. Give all the glory to Jesus.

"Man shall not live by bread alone; but man lives by every word that proceeds from the mouth of the LORD. Therefore you shall keep the commandments of the LORD your God, to walk in His ways and to fear Him" (Deut. 8:4b, 6).

Are we living for the Lord or living for the world? Never stop falling in love with Jesus. Live every day as His ambassadors. The one person you choose not to witness to might die that night and never get the opportunity to hear about the Lord; he will be lost forever.

Jesus paid a big price for you. What are you giving Him in return? Give Him your life. He wants you to be His ambassador. Serve the Lord.

2

Purpose of Life

To learn the purpose of life, you must get into the Word of God and study it daily. Cling to Him, ask Him, "What do You have for me personally?"

The purpose of our life is to worship and serve the Lord. It is as simple as that.

One day every knee will bow, and every tongue will confess that Jesus is Lord. To be a Christian is not just lip service, we all are part of the Great Commission. We must open the Bible, live what we read and serve our God. That is what life is all about.

We must consecrate ourselves unto the Lord. We must hunger for God's Word.

Did you ever think…well, here I am, now what? Do you know that the Creator of all things, the Almighty God, has a plan for you? He does, and all we have to do is ask Him what you can do for Him how He can use you. How awesome is that! For the Lord to actually use someone as small as ourselves. He has used fishermen; He can use you and will if you will ask Him in prayer. He gave us all a choice to make in our lives; we can ignore Him and live our own life or use our lives to bring glory to God, to be used as His tool to further His kingdom. How awesome! What an undeserving honor and privilege! And all we have to do is ask.

God's purpose for your life is peace and light. Do not waste your life in darkness. You must love the Lord your God more than anyone else, more than your own life.

We all are to serve the Lord; serving Him is not just set-aside for some people. The Lord wants all of us to serve Him.

The Lord says, "Therefore whoever does not practice righteousness is not of God."

Life is not about us; it is all about Christ.

When life seems boring, remember the Lord. "But it is written; Eye has not seen nor ear heard nor have entered into the heart of man the things which God has prepared for those who love Him" (1 Cor. 2:9).

Yes, God has plans for you if you love Him. All you have to do is ask Him with all of your heart.

What is the purpose of life? It is to serve the Lord.

"And do not be conformed to this world, but be transformed by the renewing of your mind, that you may prove what is that good and acceptable and perfect will of God" (Rom. 12:2).

Search for a personal relationship with the Lord Jesus Christ, and you will be eternally thankful you did. Do not look back; your commitment is not there. Being fit to serve Him is a commitment; prepare to take up your cross and follow the Lord.

You will not glorify God much unless you really put all you have into the ways of the Lord. This is what life is all about, our work for the Lord Jesus Christ.

No, life is not all about you; it is about a personal relationship with the creator of all things. We were created to serve Him. He must be number one in our life.

"That you may love the LORD your God, that you may obey His voice and that you may cling to Him, for He is your life and the length of your days" (Deut. 30:20a).

Love the Lord your God, listen to God and cling to Him. We are to love Him, adore Him, and search for His leading in our life. We are to pay attention to what He says in the Scriptures and cling to Him. God speaks today to His people. He never stopped speaking to us.

We should strive to hear those wonderful words from the Lord on the day He brings us home. "Well done My faithful servant, come into your inheritance." Yes! That is what life is all about.

So many people ask: What is the purpose of life? What is my purpose in this world?

Jesus tells us over and over again to follow Him, for us to turn our back on sin and totally repent. We are to bear good fruit for Him and to be His servants, to be used by the Lord to further His kingdom. That, my friend, is the purpose of life.

What is your mission in life? Are you making Jesus known in your city, where you work? Jesus tells us to go out and tell the world. There is not any greater honor than this!

We are to bless Him in the morning, noon, and night. Never take your eyes off of the Lord. Try to capture His heart like King David did with constant praise!

We want to know Jesus. Are we willing to give up everything to know Him? We are to be living our lives for Him; we are to live to serve Him.

To know the Lord and to make Him known to others should be our mission statement!

The purpose of our life is to serve the Lord! Yes, we will be going down rocky roads but we have to just keep your eyes upon Jesus, and He will carry us through and use those trials for His glory.

It is not all about you and it is not all about me. It is all about the risen Savior the Messiah, the Lord Jesus Christ. It is all about Jesus.

We were all created for a reason. Ask the Lord what road He wants you to do down to serve Him.

"Do you not know that those who run in a race all run, but one receives the prize? Run in such a way that you may obtain it. And everyone who competes for the prize is temperate in all things. Now they do it to obtain a perishable crown, but we for an imperishable crown" (1 Cor. 9:24–25).

Paul is talking about our race in our everyday lives. We are to run our lives, as in a race, with Jesus at the finish line. If we live for Him, to be used by Him as His servants, then we have a reward when we arrive at the finish line. Not a crown that will wither away, but to obtain a crown given to us by the Lord.

Jesus asks us to spend our time of waiting for His return by taking care of His children and doing His work here, both in the church and outside of it.

Our ultimate goal in life is "To know the Lord."

3

How to Live Today

In Joshua 22:5, when the Lord's people entered the Promised Land, the Lord told them how they should live: "To walk in all His ways, to obey His commands, to hold fast to Him and to serve Him with all your heart and all your soul." These commands of God never changed; we are to hold fast to these words and to live our lives to please the God of all creation.

Our failure to live according to God's expectations has caused a separation between God and us. Morally and ethically, we look like God, or at least we did when we were first created. We were designed for a relationship but found ourselves alienated from our Creator because of worldly sin.

For us to get back to God:

1. We must read and study the Word of God daily and live what we read.
2. We must get into a strong prayer life not only in the morning/night, but without ceasing throughout your day.
3. We must attend a good Bible teaching church. (I recommend a Baptist Church.)

4. Attend Sunday school to learn the scripture so you can live and share what you learn.

5. Attend the Worship service to worship the Lord with all of your heart along with other saints of the Lord.

6. Learn from the services and live what you learn.

"For the wages of sin is death, but the gift of God is eternal life in Christ Jesus our Lord" (Rom. 6:23).

In Scripture, death is eternal separation from God. The big question is, did you turn your back on your sins to please God? Or are you still living in sin accepted by the world but being rejected by God? Are you living with your girlfriend/boyfriend because the world says it is okay? This, my friend, is sin and displeasing to God but glorifying Satan. My question is: whom do you serve by your lifestyle? The wages of sin is death.

Stand strong upon the Lord today.

"This is the day the LORD has made; we will rejoice and be glad in it" (Ps. 118:24).

No matter what the day will bring, be happy, because the Lord made this day for you!

If you are in the workplace, you do not work for the "man," you are to work very hard to glorify Jesus through your work; you work for Him.

Do not forget to read the Word of the Lord before you leave the house! Start the day off right. Witness, witness, and then witness some more.

Protect us, O Lord, from the evil one today. Be glorified through us today.

I just want to bring you some words of caution. If cupid shoots an arrow at you, remember: If we are followers of Jesus, then the Holy Spirit dwells within us, our bodies are a temple of the Holy Spirit.

"Do you not know that your body is the temple of the Holy Spirit who is in you, whom you have from God and you are not your own?" (1 Cor. 6:19).

Do not let anyone defile the Lord's temple, which is your body! Also, if your new friend does *not* love Jesus, then Satan will use that person to draw you away from Jesus. The Lord tells us not to be unequally yoked. Please do not let this happen to you. And finally, if your new friend does love Jesus like you do, go to church with her/him and grow in the Lord together. The Lord will be blessed!

Stand strong upon the Lord; do not let Satan hold you back! Show the world today whose side you are on. Do not forget to read the Word of the Lord before you leave the house.

Today is the day the Lord has made; let us serve Him with all of our heart and strength today. Let us show Satan whose side we are on!

Be careful whom you push out of your life; the diversity of others was designed to perfect and complete you.

Jesus gave his all for us; we need to offer Him our all. Serve Him with all of your heart today. Make him proud!

Keep your eyes focused only upon the Lord today! Let Him be glorified with everything you do and say it. Bless Him at all times.

Let us try as hard as we can to make Jesus proud of us today! Touch the heart of our Lord with our services unto Him. What an honor.

Stay strong in the Lord; serve Him with all of your heart today. Tell everyone you see today why you love Him so much.

Our God is an awesome God; let us serve Him with all of our hearts today! He is so deserving.

Jesus, Jesus, only Jesus should be your vocal point in your life. Show the world whose side you are on.

4

The World

Guard jealously your relationship with God. If you are depending upon anything other than Jesus, you will never know when He is gone.

The Lord does not change; we are the ones who change. Do not become contaminated like the world.

The government turns their back on God and His laws, and when everything goes haywire and disaster happens they cry, "Where is God?"

You cannot effectively make a difference for Christ when you have the same mindset as the world. You must be transformed.

We can live like the world, or we can live like we belong to Jesus. If we belong to Jesus, we are to be His reflection always; we are to be His ambassadors. We all have a choice. Jesus promises us eternal life with Him forever—the world promises you nothing.

There is so much sin in this world, and people are turning from the Word of God to the words of man. We must always remember this: the wrath of God will be poured out on this world. God will protect His loyal servants. Jesus said that the world would hate you. It is okay, let them. We belong to Jesus!

Read His writings and pray always throughout the day and never take your eyes off of our risen Savior the Lord Jesus Christ. Let Him lead and guide you, not the world.

We must take our eyes off of the world and its sinfulness and focus upon being the person God created us to be. We must draw close to Him and to serve Him. This is such an undeserving honor. The reward is eternal life with Him. How wonderful!

When you spend so much time around worldly people, you become like them. Get back into reading the Scriptures daily and get back into that close relationship with the Lord you once had. You will be so much happier.

You like the world, but still want to please the Lord. Jesus says that He will not tolerate this. He wants all of you. He does not take pleasure in lukewarm followers. Who are we to be faithful to? Are we to be loyal to the world or the Creator of all things, the Almighty God? It's time for some soul searching.

"You are of God, little children, and have overcome them, because He who is in you is greater that he who is in the world" (1 John 4:4).

When the world seems out of control, just focus upon your Savior Jesus; He is in total control.

Therefore, whoever does not practice righteousness is not of God.

The world is so dark; we must be the light of the world. Let Jesus shine through you.

Do not just act like you love the Lord and live as the world does. Live the Word of God, not the word of man, which is in serious error.

"Do not love the world or the things in the world. If anyone loves the world, the love of the Father is not in him. For all that is in the world, the lust of the flesh, the lust of the eyes and the pride of life is not of the Father but is of the world. And the world is passing away and the lust of it; but he who does the will of God abides forever" (1 John 2:15–17).

Everything in this world is against the way God sees things, we are lured and seduced into it. We are living in an immoral world. It is not okay! The Holy Spirit will show that the world is wrong!

"And do not be conformed to this world, but be transformed by the renewing of your mind, that you may prove what is that good and acceptable and perfect will of God" (Rom. 12:2).

The world will hate us, but remember it hated Jesus first.

Too much of the world has crept into the church, homes, and families. We fail to stop sin from coming into our homes. We are spending less time in the Bible and more time reading secular books and watching and listening to corruption on the airwaves. We are being influenced by the world and the media and not by the Lord. The wrath of God will be brought upon this world; God will protect His loyal servants.

Remember, we are just visiting this earth. We are born for a divine purpose. We are special. We have been created in the image of God! Glory to God!

This world is temporary; we are to live for eternity. As Jesus promises, if we serve Him we, will be where He is forever.

Condemnation does come to the world through Christ, because the world rejects Him. That was not part of God's purpose in sending Jesus. The Lord's goal was to save the world.

This world is getting further and further away from the Word of God. How are cursing, listening to and telling dirty jokes, lying, selfishness, deception, and drinking, premarital sex, and sexual immorality glorifying the Lord?

"Do you not know that the unrighteous will not inherit the kingdom of God? Do not be deceived, neither fornicators, nor idolaters, nor adulterers, nor homosexuals nor sodomites, nor thieves, nor covetous, nor drunkards, nor revilers, nor extortioners will inherit the kingdom of God" (1 Cor. 6:9–10).

If you are doing these things, then according to the Word of God, you do not belong to Him.

Read Scripture. It tells you what pleases the Almighty God who created all things and what is disgusting to Him.

If you are not serving the Lord in your life, then you are serving Satan. The Lord tells us that there is not any in between. Jesus is going to come quickly; we must all be ready. Do not be left behind because of worldly lust and pleasures. The Lord promises us who live for Him eternal life with Him forever. Those who live in the world and serve Satan, He promises damnation. Is it worth it? Keep your eyes focused upon the Lord always; never take your eyes off of Jesus the Messiah.

You can decide to live in the sinful world and not for Christ; that is your choice. Remember that you will perish unless you look away from human teachers and your own sinful condition to the bleeding Savior. The only reason Jesus died on the cross was so you could look to Him in faith and be saved from your sins. The gospel is for all of us.

Do not hang around with worldly people; they will just bring you down to their level, and you will end up backsliding. Do not give Satan the victory!

If you are having trouble in this world, rejoice! Our next world is trouble free and eternal!

Do not become like the world. Jesus and only Jesus will help us to overcome the world!

Christ will give you rest from all of your dreams of worldly ambition, but set a fire within you with a higher ambition than ever. Call upon Him and follow the Lord.

This worldly life is temporary, but what we do with it determines our eternity.

Has Christ come to give in to your lusts and let you do the work of Satan and then receive the wonderful wages of the godly?

No. There must be a clean sweep, an about face of the old nature to make room for the new person in Christ. We are not to be conformed to this world, if we belong to Jesus.

Contamination is out there all the time; we must stay clean and pure.

Remember, we are not of this world. So it is only reasonable that we do not see and perceive things the way nonbelievers do; stay strong in Him!

The Lord says: "Behold, I stand at the door and knock." Are you having so much fun in the world that you will not open the door? Say yes to the Lord!

Does the world hate you because of your stand for Jesus? Yes! That is great! Keep up the good work! Jesus tells us that this would happen! Stand strong upon the solid rock of our Lord.

People may talk about you behind your back, which is okay; they did the same to Jesus. That is where they belong, behind your back!

We are living in a fast-paced world. We must slow down. Do not miss some of the blessings the Lord has for you.

Do not follow the commandments of man, the world. Follow the commandments of God.

5

Unbelief

There are some who do not yet know Christ. If you are troubled with unbelief, believe as much as you can and then cry out to the Lord.

"Jesus said to him. If you can believe, all things are possible to him who believes. Immediately the father of the child cried out and said with tears. Lord, I believe; help my unbelief!" (Mark 9:23–24).

Make sure you take down any worldly walls that you might have around you, be teachable and ask the Lord to teach you more.

Unbelief is a choice one has made. If you were in a burning house, you would be eager to get out of it. If there seemed a probability that you would sink in a river, you would struggle desperately to get to shore. Why do you have very little concern for your very soul then?

We are so unworthy of the Lord, but still He knows who we are and loves us more than anyone ever can. We are washed in His blood and covered in His righteousness. We are but a single grain of sand in the middle of the Sahara Desert and still He knows us by name. How amazing!

6

Sin

Remember, we must not be deceived by our sins; you must turn your back on them or Jesus will have nothing to do with you.

The only cure for sin is to look in faith to the Savior, who was lifted up on a cross when He died in our place became sin for us.

"But God demonstrates His own love toward us, in that while we were still sinners, Christ died for us" (Rom. 5:8).

"As far as the east is from the west, so far has He removed our transgressions from us" (Ps. 103:12).

There is so much sin in this world and people are turning from the Word of God to the words of man. We must always remember this: the wrath of God will be poured out on this world. God will protect His loyal servants.

Lives have to change. Truly knowing the Lord means we are being changed by Him on a daily basis. People think they know the Lord but really do not. You cannot really know Him if your sin has not been totally removed.

"Therefore do not let sin reign in your mortal body, that you should obey it in its lusts. And do not present your members as instruments of unrighteousness to sin. But present yourselves to God being alive from the dead and your members as instruments of righteousness to God" (Rom. 6:12–13).

Change yourselves to be dead indeed to sin, but alive to God in Christ Jesus our Lord.

Do not be overcome by evil, but overcome evil with good.

"He who sins is of the devil, for the devil has sinned from the beginning. For this purpose the Son of God was manifested that He might destroy the works of the devil" (1 John 3:8).

This world is so dark; we must be the light of the world. Let Jesus shine through you. Remember he who sins is of the devil, for the devil has sinned from the beginning.

"If we say that we have no sin, we deceive ourselves, and the truth is not in us. If we confess our sins, He is faithful and just to forgive us our sins and to cleanse us from all unrighteousness" (1 John 1:8–9).

"For all have sinned and fall short of the glory of God" (Rom. 3:23).

"But if we walk in the light as He is in the light, we have fellowship with one another, and the blood of Jesus Christ His Son cleanses us from all sin" (1 John 1:7).

Walking in the light means, we are to be a reflection of Christ; we are to be holy for He is holy.

Whoever abides in Jesus does not sin. Whoever sins does not know the Lord.

We are to be "dead to sin and alive in Christ.

Everyone who sins is a slave to sin.

Since Christ freed us from our sins by His blood, we must hate sin. It murdered our Lord! It cost Him His life to save us. How, then, are we to toy with it? We are freed from our sins. Sin no longer holds us captive. The blood of the Lord dissolves the chains.

My question is then, how can we go about as if we were still slaves to it?

"For the wages of sin is death, but the gift of God is eternal life in Christ Jesus our Lord" (Rom. 6:23).

Turn your back on Satan, and he will flee from you. That is a promise!

Do you know that those who love their sin cannot love the Savior? They must love the one and hate the other. It is a terrible choice when people reject Christ, who is light and choose the outer darkness of sin.

There are times when Satan gets the best of us, and we end up in sin. King David knew this very well. He cried out unto the Lord in Psalm 51 after he sinned with Bathsheba.

"Have mercy upon me, O God. According to Your loving-kindness; According to the multitude of Your tender mercies, blot out my transgressions. Wash me thoroughly from my iniquity. And cleanse me from my sin.

Create in me a clean heart, O God, and renew a steadfast spirit within me. Do not cast me away from Your presence. And do not take Your Holy Spirit from me. Restore to me the joy of Your salvation and uphold me by Your generous Spirit" (Ps. 51:1–2,10–12)

If you think that, you might be sinning against God. The world will tell you that what you are doing is okay. If there is any doubt in your mind then *stop* what you are doing! It is better to stop what you are doing than spend eternity in hell with Satan and his gang. Turn your back on the world. (Satan is of the world.) Run to Jesus!

Only Jesus has the authority to forgive sin, not man! Be careful who gives your loved one their last rights! They must ask Jesus for forgiveness! Only in the name of Jesus are your sins forgiven. Not in the name of your local church. (This was a bad experience for me. Just before the Lord brought my mother home, her clergy forgave her of her sins by the power of their church. This made my skin crawl.) Again, only Jesus can forgive sins.

"The next day John saw Jesus coming toward him and said, "Behold! The Lamb of God who takes away the sin of the world!" (John 1:29).

Only through the blood of Jesus, while hanging upon the cross, our sins are totally washed away! Thank you, Jesus! Jesus freely sacrificed His life for you and for me. He promises us eternal life with Him, if we belong to Him. He is the sacrificed lamb and He washed away our sins, if we repent of them and follow Him.

Jesus is the way; He is the only way.

People of the world turn from the Word of God to the words of man, then disasters happen and they ask: "Where is God?" He always was there—we turned from Him.

We must try as hard as we can to turn our back on sin, whenever we sin; we glorify Satan, not God.

Sin is the source of the world's brokenness.

"O God, You know my foolishness; and my sins are not hidden from You" (Ps. 69:5).

We must never think that our sins are hidden; the Lord knows them well.

Sin cools your love for God and others, by turning your focus on yourself.

The word *death*, in the Bible, means eternal separation from the Lord. How devastating is that!

If you think: I am okay, I lived a good life and I am a good person. Remember the words of the Lord: "As it is written: There is none righteous, no not one" (Rom. 3:10).

We are either for Jesus or against Him.

"He who is not with Me is against Me" (Matt. 12:30a).

There is no other way!

"He who says, I know Him and does not keep His commandments, is a liar and the truth is not in him. But whoever keeps His Word, truly the love of God is perfected in him. By this we know that we are in Him" (1 John 2:4).

We are either for Jesus or against Him. You either live in the world or you live to serve Jesus; there is not any in-between.

We are called to be a Son of God. Do not run from the Lord; run to the Lord!

7

Despair

Do not look back…you are not going that way.

Jesus tells us not to look back, just keep on looking forward and to follow Him.

Do you sometimes feel that you do not matter to anyone, or feel hurt by the way others let you down? Jesus understands. Run to Him.

"Come to Me, all you who labor and are heavy laden and I will give you rest" (Matt. 11:28).

Jesus has the rope. Give your life to Him, and He will pull you out of your despair. You will see a bright shining light at the end of the road; run down that road, brush the dust off of your Bible and learn His Word and serve Him. That is what life is all about.

When you feel like you are all alone, Jesus promises that He will never leave you. Just call out to the Lord; He is there waiting to hear from you.

You might feel lost, confused, or depressed all the time. You do not understand why. It is like a big empty hole inside of you; and no matter what you do, it never gets filled up, it never goes away. You may try drinking it away with alcohol or with drugs, maybe other sinful acts. But nothing fills the emptiness that you have.

I am asking you to call out to Jesus. He will fill he emptiness within you; He understands. Call out to Him, and He will make you full and complete again. He will totally fill that emptiness within you with the Holy Spirit of God, and you will never be empty again. Only Jesus can help. Call out to Him with all of your heart, and He will answer you and help you.

"Whoever drinks of this water will thirst again, but whoever drinks of the water that I shall give him will never thirst. But the water that I shall give him will become in him a fountain of water springing up into everlasting life" (John 4:13–14).

Stand upon the solid rock of the Lord and He will pull you through! Stay strong in the Lord.

Stop holding on to the things that concern you, which you cannot change. Give it to the Lord and totally "let go" of it.

Place all of your burdens onto the hands of the Lord; we must totally let go of them, then we will be set free!

God may not change your situation until first there is a change in your heart.

Unhappy? Has someone turned against you?

"Cease from anger and forsake wrath; do not fret, it only causes harm" (Ps. 37:8).

In good times and in bad times, never stop praising the Lord. The moment you stop, you start falling into a pit of depression.

Sometimes God allows us to cry tears to clear our eyes so we can see the good things ahead.

Look upon the mountains you face each day as an opportunity to grow. The Lord will use those mountains for you to help others.

The Lord is our strength and a very present help in trouble. Just call upon the Lord. He wants to hear from you; He wants to help.

Run to Jesus, do not rely on your friends—Jesus is to be our help. Go to Him and lay everything at His feet then let go!

Worry is like a rocking chair; it gives you something to do, but it does not get you anywhere. Place your trust in the Lord and let Him handle it.

Whatever the enemy steals from you, God will restore to you. Look at Job. Give Him the praise through your depressions.

There are times when people are against you, they walk all over you. You may be upset and depressed. Just keep on being a reflection of Jesus. He is the only one you are to please. No one else can promise you eternal life, no one else can ever give their life for you and if they do, their blood will not do you any good. Only the blood of Jesus washes away your sins. No one else will ever love you as much as Jesus does. Go to Him and give Him your life as He gave His for you. Read His Word daily and live what you read.

You will gain a close relationship with Him, and no one can ever take that happiness away from you.

Pain does not just show up in our lives for no reason; it is a sign that something in our lives needs to change. Take it to the Lord.

8

Choice

Choice. It is so wonderful that we all have a choice to make in living our life. We can either choose to live for Jesus and glorify Him with everything we say and do. Or we can live in the world and glorify Satan in everything we say and do. Jesus tells us that there is not any in-between. Those who love their sin cannot love the Savior. They must love the one and hate the other. It is a terrible choice when people reject Christ, who is light, and choose the outer darkness of sin.

"So then, because you are lukewarm and neither cold nor hot, I will vomit you out of My mouth" (Rev. 3:16).

Whatever you choose to obey becomes your master. You can choose sin, which leads to death, or you can choose to obey God and receive His approval.

Are we bearing good fruit for the Lord? Who are you serving? Jesus tells us that we cannot serve two masters.

"No one can serve two masters; for either he will hate the one and love the other, or else he will be loyal to the one and despise the other, you cannot serve God and mammon" (Matt. 6:24).

You either live for Him or you are living for Satan. You have the choice to make. The Lord gives all of us the choice, the free will to live for Him or to live for Satan; there is not any in-between.

Do you tell the people in your life about Jesus? That is a choice you have to make.

"Therefore whoever confesses Me before men, him I will also confess before My Father who is in heaven. But whoever denies Me before men, him I will also deny before my Father who is in heaven" (Matt. 10:32–33).

If we follow the Lord, then we are commanded by Jesus to go out into the world and proclaim the good news. He also said if we do not tell others about Him, then he will not tell the Father in heaven about you. He gave us a freedom of choice.

"This is a faithful saying: For if we died with Him, we shall also live with Him. If we endure, we shall also rein with Him. If we deny Him, He also will deny us" (2 Timothy 2:11–12).

Be careful. Die with Him, live with Him, reign with Him. It does not get any simpler than that. Living in the world is denying the Lord; do not let this happen to you.

Always remember: you cannot get into heaven on someone else's apron strings. Be very careful how you live your life; how you spend eternity is up to you and you alone. You have the choice to make.

> You will know them by their fruits. Do men gather grapes from thorn bushes or figs from thistles? Even

so, every good tree bears good fruit, but a bad tree bears bad fruit. A good tree cannot bear bad fruit, nor can a bad tree bear good fruit. Every tree that does not bear good fruit is cut down and thrown into the fire. Therefore by their fruits you will know them. (Matt. 7:16–20)

The Lord says, "They will know you by your fruits." You love the Lord and serve Him, but you have another side. You still hang around with unsaved friends with unclean spirits. You might say: the Lord understands, I like going to worldly concerts, and I have so much fun with unsaved friends.

Remember, someone is always watching. You might decide to go have a few drinks with your unsaved coworkers on a Friday night after work, and the person you might have been witnessing to the day before could be in that lounge and see you. There goes your testimony for the Lord. Make the right choice. Bear good fruit for the Lord.

What an awesome God we have. He wants us to serve Him to be used as His ambassadors to expand His kingdom; we can continue to live our lives in the sinful world, or we can make a U-turn in our life and serve the Almighty God. We all have a choice.

There are people who choose to stay impure in sin. Do not let this be you.

The moment we stop reading His Word is when we start losing sight of Him. He does not move from us; we move from Him. Choose to make it a habit in your daily life to read His Word and to live it everyday.

Are we living our lives to please ourselves, or are we living our lives for Jesus, to further His kingdom? Live your life for Jesus, and He promises you eternal life with Him forever. We all have a choice to make.

We are all on a journey in life. We have a choice as to which road to go down. Jesus is calling…

To live for Jesus, we must bury our own will and live for Him. Choose Him.

Remember Noah's Ark? Do not wait until tomorrow to come to Jesus, tomorrow might be too late. Do not miss the boat!

9

Comfort

It is such a comfort to have a personal relationship with the Lord; without it, we are like lost sheep that have gone astray.

"Then you will call and the LORD will answer; you will cry for help and He will say: Here am I" (Isa. 58:9a).

Put your trust in the Lord, He is our portion now and forever. In good times and in bad, the Lord is in control. Run to Him!

When the world seems out of control, just focus upon your Savior. Jesus is always there and in total control.

Do not try to understand, just trust in the Lord with all of your heart.

You can either let life knock you down, or you can stand up on the solid rock of Jesus and let Him take over.

"Cease from anger and forsake wrath; do not fret, it only causes harm" (Ps. 37:8).

Who are we but a speck of dust, still, the Lord knows us by name. Amazing!

Expect the Lord to move in your life, and He will move!

We must get out of the darkness and into the light; Jesus is the light. He wants you to come to Him; He wants to help you with whatever you are going through.

Man can give you false hopes. The Lord loves you enough to give His life for you. Run to Jesus.

Jesus tells us not to be afraid, that He is with us always. When you think you are alone, you are not. He will never leave you, just call out to Him; He is there waiting to hear from you.

Did someone do something against you? The Lord says, "Vengeance is Mine" (Deut. 32:35a).

Just let it go and give it to the Lord.

Set your mind on things above, not on things on the earth.

My home is in heaven. I'm just traveling through this world.

We cannot handle what life brings to us alone. We need help; we need a personal relationship with Jesus the Messiah.

Do you feel discouraged or alone? Jesus has been there; go to Him.

You keep on sharing your problems with people; that shows your lack of trust in God. Run to the Lord, not your friends.

When it looks like the sky is falling down around you, it's okay. The Lord is in control. He will not make you go through more than you can take.

Throughout our lives, we go through so much turmoil, and we tend to run to our best friend. Run to Jesus and only Jesus.

"I will say of the Lord, He is my refuge and my fortress; My God, in Him I will trust" (Ps. 91:2).

Let the Lord be your refuge, not man, not anything that is in the world. Trust only in the Lord and let Him help you. Have faith.

"My help comes from the Lord who made heaven and earth. The Lord shall preserve you from all evil; He shall preserve your soul. The Lord shall preserve your going out and your coming in from this time forth, and ever more" (Ps. 121:1, 7–8).

King David knew very well where his help comes from and we are to learn from him. Look unto the Lord for help and only the Lord.

Christ is the missing piece of the puzzle of life that you have sought for so long. Satan would have you fight against this truth till you die.

Just as Jesus had to overcome the cross, we must overcome our cross. The only way for us to overcome our cross is to keep our eyes only upon Jesus.

Why did this have to happen to you? Ask the Lord and wait for His answer, you will be at peace thereafter.

We have all made mistakes in our lives, Jesus tells us to not look back, to just keep your eyes looking forward.

Never forget the Lord is always with you; you can handle the problems together. He is such a comfort!

"Come to Me, all you who labor and are heavy laden and I will give you rest" (Matt. 11:28).

Stop going to all your friends to find peace; you never will obtain it. Jesus promises you peace that can only come from God.

"Peace I leave with you, My peace I give to you; not as the world gives do I give to you. Let not your heart be troubled, neither let it be afraid" (John 14:27).

We have an Almighty God that never leaves us. Stay in constant communication with Him. He is near, just reach out to Him.

We need hope and Jesus is our hope.

"He heals the brokenhearted and binds up their wounds. He counts the number of the stars; He calls them all by name. Great is our Lord and mighty in power; His understanding is infinite" (Ps. 147:3–5).

We can cry, why did the Lord have this happen to me? Do not try to understand the ways of the Lord they are much too great. Just trust in the Lord with all of your heart. We could never understand the ways of the Lord.

Let go and let God.

The Lord said that everyone would hate you because of Me.

When the world seems out of control, just focus upon your Savior, Jesus is always there and in total control.

"He will fulfill the desire of those who fear Him; He also will hear their cry and save them. The LORD preserves all who love Him" (Ps. 145:19–20a).

Jesus says that he that follows Me shall not walk in darkness.

Make Jesus the source of your healing. Talk the talk and walk the walk. You might have tried everything else... try Jesus.

"Eye has not seen, nor ear heard, nor have entered into the heart of man the things which God has prepared for those who love Him" (1 Cor. 2:9).

God who is perfect in every way has prepared something for us that we have never seen; we have never heard about it. It is something we have never even thought about because our human mind does not have the ability to comprehend such things. What has God prepared for us? I know where it will come from. I know why we will receive it. It will come from the love of God when we get to heaven then we will be able to understand it. For now, we can glorify Him in the cross and what Jesus did for us there. All those in God's kingdom will understand it when we get there. But as for now, our God is so great it is impossible to try to understand the ways of the Lord.

The Lord does not want us to worry. Cast your cares upon Him. Go to Him, and He will give you rest. He will help you just ask.

Our God is a God who restores. He will restore you!

Job spoke rightly unto the Lord. The Lord restored Job's fortunes.

Greater is He that is in us than he that is in the world. Blessed is the Lord!

When we serve the Lord, we will need comfort, and Jesus is our comfort.

We are weak, but He is strong! Lean upon our Lord and give Him all of your concerns.

> The Lord is my shepherd; I shall not want. He makes me to lie down in green pastures; He leads me beside the still waters, He restores my soul; He leads me in the paths of righteousness for His name's sake. Yea, though I walk through the valley of the shadow of death, I will fear no evil; for You are with me; Your rod and Your staff, they comfort me. You prepare a table before me in the presence of my enemies; You anoint my head with oil; my cup runs over. Surely goodness and mercy shall follow me all the days of my life; and I will dwell in the house of the Lord Forever. (Ps. 23)

The Lord is our shepherd; let Him lead you and comfort you. Do not lean upon man. Jesus and only Jesus is our peace, shelter, solid rock, and fortress.

Are you close to the Lord? Does His rod and staff comfort you? If not, you need to draw closer to the Lord through the Bible and prayer.

We are so small and weak, but still the Lord knows us by name. He knows the number of hairs upon our head. What an awesome God we have!

Continue to give glory to God in your suffering, and He will restore you. You will be strong in the Lord.

Try not to take things personally what people say about you. The only one you are to please is the Lord!

Do not worry; worrying shows a lack of faith in God. Be strong and focus upon the Lord.

God does not ignore those who depend on Him.

"Bless be the God and Father of our Lord Jesus Christ, the Father of mercies and God of all comfort" (2 Cor. 1:3).

10

Hope

We need hope, and Jesus is hope.

"The Lord is near to those who have a broken heart and saves such as have a contrite spirit" (Ps. 34:18).

When it looks like the sky is falling down around you, it is okay. The Lord is in control! He will not make you go through more than you can take. Cling to Jesus!

All of us go through troubled times. Those troubled times should bring us into a closer relationship with the Lord. It is good to just fall into the arms of Jesus. Sometimes people go in the other direction. Then they ask: Where is He? Why isn't the Lord helping me? Why has He deserted me? I'm all-alone and in a pit, I really need a rope to pull me out.

The question we should be asking ourselves: Are we focusing only upon the Lord? Are we praying with a sincere heart? Is our focus off of the sinful world, and are our eyes focused upon the Lord's direction for us. If we are not looking for the Lord's leading with a pure heart, we will not see the rope He has sent down to pull you up.

The Lord did not promise us a bed of roses. The world will hate us, and this is okay, because we have a great inheritance with the Lord.

We have to know our God as a God who restores. He will restore. Stand strong upon the hope of the Lord.

"Delight yourself also in the LORD and He shall give you the desires of your heart, commit your way to the LORD, trust also in Him and He shall bring it to pass" (Ps. 37:4–5).

When all hope is lost, look only to the savior, the Lord Jesus Christ. Jesus is our only hope. Run to Him with all of your heart.

11

Peace

With whatever we are going through. Place it into the hands of the Lord, He promises us peace that is beyond all understanding.

"Peace I leave with you, My peace I give to you; not as the world gives do I give to you. Let not your heart be troubled neither let it be afraid" (John 14:27).

Jesus tells us not to let our hearts be troubled; He is talking to you and to me. Jesus wants us to be in total peace in Him.

We have an Almighty God that never leaves us. Stay in constant communication with Him, He is near, just reach out.

"Come to Me, all you who labor and are heavy laden and I will give you rest" (Matt. 11:28).

Stop going to all of your friends to find peace, you never will obtain it. Jesus promises you peace that can only come from God and God alone.

"God has called us to peace" (1 Cor. 7:15b).

He has called "us" to peace. That is for you and me. We just have to claim it. Run to the Lord and claim the peace that He has promised to you.

Paul writes to the Corinthian church: "Finally brethren, farewell. Become complete. Be of good comfort, be of one mind, live in peace; and the God of love and peace will be with you" (2 Cor. 13:11).

Yes, the comfort and the God of love and peace is not just for the people of the Corinthian church, it is for you and me also. We have a God that promises us great peace. Run to Him, run into the arms of the Lord, you will have peace in abundance.

"But now in Christ Jesus you who once were far off have been brought near by the blood of Christ. For He Himself is our peace" (Eph. 2:13–14a).

There is unconditional love and great peace in Jesus.

"The LORD bless you and keep you; The LORD make His face shine upon you and be gracious to you: The LORD lift up His countenance upon you and give you peace" (Numbers 6:24–26).

Amen and amen.

12

Refuge

Blessed is he who takes refuge in Him.

"Hear my cry, O God; attend to my prayer. From the end of the earth I will cry to You, when my heart is overwhelmed; lead me to the rock that is higher than I. For You have been a shelter for me, a strong tower from the enemy. I will abide in Your tabernacle forever; I will trust in the shelter of Your wings."(Ps. 61:1–4).

Yes, just like David, cry unto the Lord, run to Him. The Lord is our refuge. Thank you Jesus!

"God is our refuge and strength, a very present help in trouble" (Ps. 46:1).

He is your refuge and He is your strength. We must not just read the bible we must live it. We must learn the Word of God and apply it to our own lives!

"The Lord also will be a refuge for the oppressed, a refuge in times of trouble. And those who know Your name will put their trust in You; For You, Lord, have not forsaken those who seek You" (Ps. 9:9–10).

Do you sometimes feel that you do not matter to anyone or feel hurt by the way others let you down? Jesus understands, run to Him.

Stand strong upon the solid rock of Jesus! He alone is your refuge and your strength, your help in trouble.

Stand strong upon the Word of the Lord.

When everyone turns against you, remember the Lord is always with you, He promises that He will never leave you. Praise the Lord!

"Be still and know that I am God" (Ps. 46:10a).

Yes! The Lord tells us to just stop, to take a step back. To be still and know that He is God, He is in control of all things.

Throughout our lives, we go through so much turmoil. Who do you turn to? Let it be the Lord. He is the only one who really understands and the only one who can give you total peace. Let it be Jesus.

Let the Lord be your refuge, not man, not anything that is in the world. Trust only in the Lord of all creation, the Creator of all things. Let Him help you. Have faith.

We all make mistakes in our lives. We are to be like King David when he would call out unto the Lord: "Be merciful to me, O God, be merciful to me! For my soul trusts in You; and in the shadow of Your wings I will make my refuge until these calamities have passed by. I will cry out to God Most High" (Ps. 57:1–2a).

Cry out to the Lord God Almighty. Cry out, "Be merciful to me O Lord!" He will hear you and He will help you.

"But the LORD has been my defense, and my God the rock of my refuge" (Ps. 94:22).

Remember, man cannot help you like the Lord can. Man can turn against you or give you false hopes. The Lord loves you enough to give His life for you.

13

Faith

Your faith can bless others as well as yourself. It not only comforts your own heart, but also enables you to speak words of love to others.

Trust in the Lord and only the Lord. Do not try to understand where the Lord is leading you. Just go and honor Him. It is between you and Him only.

Genuine faith means bearing fruit for God's kingdom. The just shall live by faith

Do not worry; worrying shows a lack of faith and understanding in God. Be strong and focus upon the Lord.

Let us get into fellowship with Christ, give ourselves to Him without reserve, and see life in an eternal light, looking ahead to the reward. Obedience of faith is to keep your eyes on the Lord at all times and just have Him lead you.

We must all stand strong upon the solid rock of our Lord! He alone is our rock, our salvation, and our refuge. Blessed is the Lord!

Jesus is our example of a faithful servant.

"For I know that my Redeemer lives. And He shall stand at last on the earth" (Job 19:25).

When you would go through a bad tribulation. Never stop praising the Lord! Let the rock of ages be praised. Let it be said that your faith is strong and it did not falter; it was built upon the solid rock of Jesus Christ.

Noah came into the ark with his wife, sons, and their wives. Their obedience was unquestioning. We do not find them asking anything at all about the reason for the command. They came as they were told. They passed through the doorway and they were all in the ark. We are not to ask the Lord why. Like Noah, we are to just go in faith and follow His lead.

To believe and have faith in Him, to love Him with all your heart and to obey His leading just as Noah and his family obeyed. That is what the Lord wants from all of us. Not just Noah and his family, you and me also. When Satan tells you to forget about the Lord and live your own life to please yourself; turn your back on him and he will flee from you, and then follow the Lord. You will be blessed.

Faith can do what unbelief must not try to do. When unbelief tries to follow in the footsteps of faith, it becomes its own destroyer. You must have real faith in God, or you cannot go where the Lord will take you to serve Him.

By faith you can go through the ocean and find yourself safe on the other side. This is the difference between faith and unbelief. Faith goes through the ocean; unbelief is drowned in the ocean.

Just as Abraham did not know where he was going, God knew, and that was enough for him. We are not to ask for full knowledge before we obey the Lord's will. We must follow the leading of the Lord in the dark just as Abraham did. We need to have strong faith.

Faith has condemning power toward an ungodly world. You do not need to be telling worldly people they are doing wrong. Let them see clearly the evidence of your life, it will bear the strongest witness against their unbelief and sin.

"For as the body without the spirit is dead, so faith without works is dead also" (James 2:26).

Faith without works is not faith at all, but a simple lack of obedience to God.

If you belong to Jesus, your life does not belong to you anymore because you have been bought with a price. To act like your life is yours will never work. In faith, let go and follow where He will lead you.

Even though we never saw Jesus, by faith we believe in Him, we believe He physically rose from the dead and we know that our Messiah is coming back soon!

Look at the things around you, and the things, which are not seen. Believe and have faith in the Lord.

"Now the just shall live by faith; but if anyone draws back, My soul has no pleasure in him" (Heb. 10:38).

Never draw back from witnessing! Have faith.

We always have to remember: greater is He that is in us than he that is in the world. Be strong and stand upon the solid rock of ages, the Lord Jesus Christ.

If you have a problem, you keep on praying and the Lord seems so far away. You must totally let go of the problem and give it totally to the Lord in faith.

The easy way is not always the godly way. Have faith in the Lord.

God has ventured all in Jesus to save us. Now He wants us to venture our all in "total abandonment" in Him. There are spots where that faith has not worked in us yet, places untouched by the life of God. There were none of those spots in Jesus Christ's life. And there are to be none in ours.

Wherever God may lead you, if you do not know where you are going, at least you know with whom you are going. You do not know the road, but you know the guide. You must have faith and be strong to breakthrough your comfort zone and go!

"But without faith it is impossible to please Him, for he who comes to God must believe that He is and that He is a rewarder of those who diligently seek Him" (Heb. 11:6).

Faith is one thing no Christian can do without; it would be like trying to burn a lantern without oil. If it is dark all around you, it is because the light of faith is gone.

Let us all make every effort to walk in His love, mercy, and grace. That will assure us our home with the Lord where trouble is not allowed.

Help from the book of Psalms:

- "My help comes from the Lord, the Maker of heaven and earth" (Ps. 121:2).
- "In my distress I called upon the LORD, and cried out to my God: He heard my voice from His temple. And my cry came before Him, even to His ears" (Ps. 18:6).
- "Oh LORD my God, I cried out to You and You healed me" (Ps. 30:2).
- "Our soul waits for the LORD; He is our help and our shield" (Ps. 33:20).
- "God is our refuge and strength, a very present help in trouble" (Ps. 46:1).

In His strength there is victory.

Faith is the courageous effort of your life; you fling yourself in reckless confidence on God.

Maintain your relationship to Jesus by the patience of faith.

Stay strong in the Lord. Keep your eyes focused only upon Him, and He will carry you through what you are going through. Do not rely on man!

He is with you always. Where else can we go from Him? Nowhere. Just like Jonah tried to hide from the Lord, it is impossible as He is with us always. No matter how high of a mountain we climb or how low under the sea we go, we can never hide from the Lord. Even in the darkest night, the dark is light to Him. We have an awesome God!

Yes! The Lord still speaks to us today. You need a close relationship with Him and He will speak to you just as He has spoken to Saul, Philip, Ananias, and all the other servants of the Lord. Have faith!

Is your faith strong enough? Do not wait until Satan comes around to find out.

Keep building upon your faith in our Lord.

Serving our Lord: you cannot see Him just now, you cannot understand what He is doing, but you know Him. Keep following. You will be greatly blessed.

Just as Peter took his eyes off of the Lord and sank, we will also sink if we take our eyes off of the Lord. Stay focused upon Him at all times.

Before making any decisions, bring it to the Lord. Let Him decide if that is where He wants you to be.

"For with God nothing will be impossible" (Luke 1:37).

"The righteous cry out and the LORD hears and delivers them out of all their troubles. The LORD is near to those who have a broken heart" (Ps. 34:17–18a).

We need to constantly keep building upon our faith, and remember: "I can do all things through Christ who strengthens me."(Philippians 4:13).

Without faith in the Lord, we are nothing.

Do not place your faith in man or in yourself, give it to the Lord; have faith in the Lord.

Through faith in Christ we have eternal life that will outlast the world, the sun, the moon and the stars!

You must stop sharing your problems with people that shows your lack of faith in God.

Just let it go and give it to the Lord.

The Lord was David's shepherd; He is your shepherd and mine. Let Him lead and guide you through your journey, give Him control and let go in total faith!

Faith makes men strong, not in the head, but in the heart.

The just shall live by faith.

God is in control, even during persecutions. He will not forget His people. Have faith.

"Therefore, having been justified by faith, we have peace with God through our Lord Jesus Christ, through whom also we have access by faith into this grace in which we stand and rejoice in hope of the glory of God" (Rom. 5:1–2).

When we go through hard times, count it as good. The Lord will use those times to build you up in your faith and to use you greater to bring Him honor and glory.

14

Repent

If you really have repented, you will hunger for God's Word in your life. You will be soaking up the Bible daily; you will be thirsty and hungry in it.

"Show me Your ways, O Lord; teach me Your paths. Lead me in Your truth and teach me. For You are the God of my salvation; On You I wait all the day. Remember, O Lord, Your tender mercies and Your loving kindnesses, for they are from of old. Do not remember the sins of my youth nor my transgressions; according to Your mercy remember me. For Your goodness sake, O Lord" (Ps. 25:4–7).

Seek the Lord, repent of your sins, and humble yourself unto the Lord.

We each have to do business with God.

Lives have to change. Truly knowing the Lord means we are being changed by Him on a daily basis. People think they know the Lord but really do not. We cannot really know Him if our sin has not been totally removed.

"For Your name's sake, O Lord, pardon my iniquity, for it is great" (Ps. 25:11).

Remember Noah's Ark? Do not wait until tomorrow to come to Jesus, tomorrow might be too late…do not miss the boat!

We must repent and never go back to that sin again.

"Do you not know that the unrighteous will not inherit the kingdom of God? Do not be deceived. Neither fornicators, nor idolaters, nor adulterers, nor homosexuals, nor sodomites, nor thieves, nor covetous, nor drunkards, nor revilers, nor extortioners will inherit the kingdom of God. (1 Cor. 6:9–10).

If you are in this list, you still have time to repent. But please hurry, no one knows what the next hour holds.

The Lord tells us, "Your deeds will not save you." The Lord tells us that He will clean us and give us a new heart a new spirit. We must repent and turn from our worldliness. Live for Jesus.

Perfect repentance; He will give us a new spirit and a new heart.

God's kindness leads us to repentance.

Repent and turn to the Lord with all your heart and your name will be written in the Book of Life.

"Create in me a clean heart, O God and renew a steadfast spirit within me. Do not cast me away from Your presence and do not take Your Holy Spirit from me. Restore to me the joy of Your salvation and uphold me by Your generous Spirit" (Ps. 51:10–12).

Like King David, we must cry out to the Lord and repent and never go back to that sin again.

When Jesus calls you, He calls you to die to yourself and follow Him.

We need Jesus the Messiah to set us free, to transform us in our daily lives.

To repent of your sins, put your faith in Christ, pray from your heart, and show the world the change Christ has made in you. That is being "born again."

Never turn your back on God's Word and its amazing story of redemption.

Do you hear the Lord calling out to you? Just say, "Here I am Lord. Help me to change."

You say that you belong to Him? Did your life totally change? Do you stay away from people with unclean spirits? If not, you are walking on a fence. Be careful. The Lord will not tolerate anyone walking on the fence; He wants all of you.

Be careful whom you let speak to you or give you spiritual advice. Not everyone hears from God!

Let today be a turning point in your life, to turn your back on sin to produce wonderful fruit for the Lord, as well as to never give in to that sinful nature but to be a new creation in Him.

15

Forgiveness

Only Jesus has the authority to forgive sin, not man!

So often we feel compelled to say when greatly offended, "I can forgive you, but I fear I shall never forget the wrong." God goes far beyond this, for He casts all our sins behind His back and He declares that He will not remember them against us anymore forever. Praise the Lord, through the blood of His Son the Lord Jesus Christ, all our sins are totally washed away!

Jesus tells us that if we have anything against anyone, forgive him; that our Father in heaven may also forgive us.

"And his master was angry, and delivered him to the torturers until he should pay all that was due to him. So my heavenly Father also will do to you if each of you, from his heart, does not forgive his brother his trespasses" (Matt. 18:35).

We must forgive. If you are having a hard time forgiving someone, ask the Holy Spirit for help; He will help you in Jesus name.

If we do not forgive someone who wrongs us, then how is Jesus to forgive us?

"For if you forgive men their trespasses, your heavenly Father will also forgive you. But if you do not forgive men their trespasses, neither will your Father forgive your trespasses" (Matt. 6:14–15).

Just as Jesus forgives us, we are to forgive.

"There was a certain creditor who had two debtors. One owed five hundred denarii, and the other fifty. And when they had nothing with which to repay, he freely forgave them both. Tell me, therefore which of them will love him more? Simon answered and said, I suppose the one whom he forgave more. And He said to him, you have rightly judged" (Luke 7:41–43).

The Lord tells us that we must forgive everyone!

"And be kind to one another, tenderhearted, forgiving one another, even as God in Christ forgave you" (Eph. 4:32).

"Bearing with one another and forgiving one another, if anyone has a complaint against another; even as Christ forgave you, so you also must do" (Col. 3:13).

"For you, Lord, are good and ready to forgive and abundant in mercy to all those who call upon you" (Ps. 86:5).

We pray in the Lord's Prayer for the Lord to forgive us as we forgive others.

"And forgive us our debts, as we forgive our debtors" (Matt. 6:12).

"If we confess our sins, He is faithful and just to forgive us our sins and to cleanse us from all unrighteousness" (1 John 1:9).

"And you, being dead in your trespasses and the uncircumcision of your flesh, He has made alive together with him, having forgiven you all trespasses" (Col. 2:13).

I love the Psalms. King David writes: "Create in me a clean heart, O God, and renew a steadfast spirit within me. Do not cast me away from Your presence and do not take Your Holy Spirit from me" (Ps. 51:10–11).

King David has sinned, and he cried out to the Lord for forgiveness. When we know we have sinned, like King David, we are to cry out to the Lord for forgiveness and never go back to that sin again.

16

Change

The Lord is the living God. He does not change, we do.

Church is more than a weekly chore. It should be a heart-moving experience as we open up our heart to God and let Him change us!

Christianity should not be our religion; it should be our lifestyle.

Our thoughts will fly wherever we place our treasures. It will be wise to let everything we have act as a magnet to draw us in the right direction. If our very best things are in heaven, our very best thoughts will fly in the same direction. But if our choicest possessions are on the earth, our hearts will be earthbound.

A man in Christ is not the old man purified, or the old man improved, or the old man in a better humor of the old man with additions or subtractions, or the old man dressed in gorgeous clothing. No, he is a new creature altogether; there has been a dramatic change!

As for the old man, what is to be done with him? Can he not be sobered, reformed, and made to do a useful service? No, he is crucified with Christ. The old man is to be buried deep and never dug up again. He cannot be mended, and therefore must be ended. The carnal mind is enmity against God. You cannot change the old nature; it is impossible to change. The sooner it is put away as a filthy and unclean thing, the better for us. The believer, so far as he is in Christ, is a new creation. Not the old stuff put into a new fashion or the old material worked up into an improved form, but absolutely a new creation. Can people see the change in you? Do they see a reflection of Christ in you? Is Jesus constantly glorified through using you as His tool to further His kingdom?

Read the Gospel and use the Word of God as your guidelines for living. The Gospel changes lives.

When you are old and sickly, do not regret your life outside of the Lord. Make a commitment to change your lifestyle and live for Him now!

This world is full of sin, lies, and deceit because of Satan. It is full of sorrow and depression, close friends can turn against you and a loved one can die. In this world of constant change, we have to be strong.

The only way for us to overcome the world is to have a close relationship with Jesus. This should be a daily ambition. Jesus will never let us down, will never leave us. Jesus should be number one in our lives. Having a personal relationship with Jesus will help us to climb those mountains that are before us. Let Him be your life. Turn your back on the world and the evils that are in the world and gain a close relationship with Jesus. His promises are everlasting; His peace is beyond understanding, and no one can ever love you more than Jesus. He has great plans for us; we just have to turn our back on self and follow Him.

Turn your life around; do not wait until it is too late. Jesus is coming very soon!

17

Salvation

Work out your salvation with fear and trembling. Obey the Word of God.

Seek the Lord, repent of your sins, and humble yourself unto the Lord. We each have to do business with God.

"For whoever calls on the name of the LORD shall be saved" (Rom. 10:13).

You were not saved just to keep you from hell. You have become Christ's spokesperson on earth.

If you are saved, then stand up in the gift of righteousness and leave that old mess behind. You are called to greater things!

We cannot save ourselves; the Lord will save us.

Since we put our trust in an atonement provided and apply by grace through Christ Jesus, we are no longer slaves but children, not working to be saved, but saved already and working for the Lord because we are saved.

We need a new spirit; without the new spirit, we cannot please God.

"That if you confess with your mouth the Lord Jesus and believe in your heart that God raised Him from the dead, you will be saved" (Rom. 10:9).

God's glory was poured into the baby of Bethlehem; it was all so frail and so unexpected. But it is also the light of God's glory that brightens every dark corner of our lives. Our holiday theme should be: Jesus and His mission on Earth, salvation through faith in Him.

18

Born Again

You hear people say, "You must be born again." Jesus said this to Nicodemus.

This term came from the Old Testament.

> Therefore say, thus says the Lord God: I will gather you from the peoples, assemble you from the countries where you have been scattered, and I will give you the land of Israel. And they will go there and they will take away all its detestable things and all its abominations from there. Then I will give them one heart, and I will put a new spirit within them, and take the stony heart out of their flesh and give them a heart of flesh. That they may walk in My statues and keep My judgments and do them; and they shall be My people, and I will be their God.
>
> But as for those whose hearts follow the desire for their detestable things and their abominations, I will recompense their deeds on their own heads, Says the Lord God. (Ezek. 11:17–21)

Yes, that is what it means to be "born again."

Are you acting the same way you did before you knew Jesus? If so, then you are not born again. To be born again, there has to be a change in your life.

Like in the verses in Ezekiel, we must have our hearts of stone transformed into hearts of flesh. We are to have a hunger for God and be a different person altogether, to glorify Him and to want to serve Him. That is what it is to be born again.

So many people hear the words *born again*, but they seem to discredit it. Maybe they just do not understand what Jesus was saying.

We have a higher calling. We are not to be of the world; people are to see the difference in us.

When Jesus calls you, He calls you to die to yourself and follow Him.

We all need the Messiah (Jesus) to set us free, to transform us in our daily lives.

As Christians we believe that we are born twice. We have received a new and heavenly life. My question is: what do we do more than others? We should show that there is more in us than in others, by letting more of Jesus come out of us. If we truly believe in Jesus, much more is expected of us than of the ones that are not reborn spiritually.

If the professed Christian is no better in his daily conversation than the ungodly, depend upon it; he is not born again in Christ Jesus.

Being born again, we poses a higher life, we are lifted to a nobler platform than the common man. Therefore, we must lead a nobler life and be guided by the highest moral spiritual value.

Let the children of darkness meet evil with evil and carry on their wars and fighting, their strife and envying, their malice and their revenge. But as for us, we are believers, we are the children of the God of love and we must serve the Lord with everything we say and do; we have been born again in Christ Jesus.

There has to be a "new you." We are to live the Word of God, so that it will change your life so much that people will see and comment about the change in you.

"Jesus answered and said to him. Most assuredly I say to you, unless one is born again, he cannot see the kingdom of God" (John 3:3).

"The kingdom of God" is such a mystery that our old nature cannot see, or understand it. We must have new eyes. We must be new people. We must be born again.

Do you understand that you cannot polish yourself up to a certain point and then be admitted into the kingdom of God? There must be a *radical* change in you, a new birth from heaven, if you are even to "see the kingdom of God."

We must always remember: following Jesus is not a religion; it is a relationship with Jesus Christ. We must be born again.

Some people think they are a Christian just because they know who Jesus is. Jesus tells us that we must be born again.

The real washing comes from Jesus Christ; our soul needs to be made clean, and this is only possible by the grace of the Lord.

Going to church does not make you a Christian any more than going into a garage makes you a car. How do you know if you have been born again? You will repent of your sins, put your faith in Christ, pray from your heart, and show the world the change Christ has made in you.

You may be rich or poor, but you must be born again. You may be intelligent, educated, or talented, but you must be born again. Many things are desirable, but this one thing is absolutely necessary. The Spirit of God purifies us from sin as water purifies our flesh. This takes place when we are born again.

> Most assuredly, I say to you, unless one is born of water and the Spirit, he cannot enter the kingdom of God. That which is born of the flesh is flesh, and that which is born of the Spirit is spirit. Do not marvel that I said to you, you must be born again. The wind bows where it wishes, and you hear the sound of it, but cannot tell where it comes from and where it goes. So is everyone who is born of the Spirit. (John 5–8)

If you are fed up with worldly living, turn your life around. Ask the Holy Spirit for His help and be spiritually born again, live your life not for yourself, but for the one who died on the cross in order for you to have eternal life.

Do you hear Jesus calling you? He wants you to die to yourself and follow Him.

19

Transformed

In the Genesis 22, God tested Abraham's loyalty to Him by telling him to present Isaac to the Lord as a sacrifice, as a burnt offering. Abraham took his son and went. At the last minute, before he was to slay Isaac, the Lord stopped him and presented a ram to take Isaac's place.

The same discipline goes on in our lives. God nowhere tells us to give up things for the sake of giving them up. He tells us to give them up for the sake of the only thing worth having—life with Him.

For us to let go of the things in our lives, to be set free of the chains that bound us to the world, by being identified with the death of Jesus, we enter into a relationship with God where we can sacrifice our lives to Him, to present to Him our lives as a living sacrifice of worship. This is what life is all about. This is how to please the Almighty God.

"I beseech you therefore, brethren, by the mercies of God, that you present your bodies a living sacrifice, holy, acceptable to God, which is your reasonable service. And do not be conformed to this world, but be transformed by the renewing of your mind, that you may prove what is that good and acceptable and perfect will of God" (Rom. 12:1–2).

We must be changed, to be dead indeed to sin, but alive to God in Christ Jesus.

Have you met Him? Have you been transformed? We need to be conformed and transformed in Christ, not just on Sundays but everyday.

We must change ourselves, to be dead indeed to sin, but alive to God in Christ Jesus our Lord.

Are we still living according to our old nature? Or do we have a new life in Christ Jesus?

Will you allow your life to be transformed? We must all read the Word of God daily and allow the Word of God to transform us, to set us free in our daily lives. To live for Him and not the world. We have an awesome God; be transformed by His Word, and we will have an eternal inheritance with Him forever.

A seed has to die to produce. We are to die to ourselves (to our old nature) to become a new creation for the Lord to use us to further His kingdom.

There are many who claim to be Christians and believers, but they have never experienced any change that they can remember from when they were a child. Well, my friend, there must be a big change if you are a Christian. I will not say that you need to know the day and the hour, but depend upon it. If you are now what you were when you were young, you are in the bond of iniquity. If there has not been a turning point in your lifestyle, you are going the wrong way. We must be turned from the way in which we were when we were born, or we are facing sin and destruction. We must be turned right around so as to have our faces towards holiness and everlasting life. Where is not such a turning point, it is time for heart-searching, humiliation, and for the seeking of salvation. Have you undergone a great transformation? Do your friends and relatives see you and ask what is so different about you?

We need to live by the Lord's rules. We have to be changed from the inside out. Are you a reflection of Christ? This should be our constant goal if we really belong to Him. We have an awesome God. To be transformed by His Word, we will have an eternal inheritance with Him forever.

If we belong to the Lord, then we must be His servants; we must not be carnal. Do not let yourself be conformed to the world, but be conformed to the Lord for you cannot be living in the flesh, transform your mind by God's Word. Let the Word of God change your life.

Every man must be turned from the way in which you were when you were born or you are facing sin and destruction, we must be turned right around so as to have our faces towards holiness and everlasting life. Where there is not such a turning, there is a great need for heart-searching, humiliation and for the seeking of salvation. Have you undergone a great transformation?

"Therefore, if anyone is in Christ, he is a new creation; old things has passed away; behold all things have become new" (2 Cor. 5:17).

Take a look at your past; are you a totally different person? Do people see a change in you for the better? Do they see Christ Jesus in you?

"Therefore you shall be perfect, just as your Father in heaven is perfect" (Matt. 5:48).

This verse is something we are to daily strive for.

The expression of Christian character is not doing good deeds, but God-likeness. If the Spirit of God has transformed you within, you will exhibit divine characteristics in your life, not good human characteristics.

We must be renewed by the Lord to be transformed into something new by the Lord. You cannot effectively make a difference for Christ when you have the same mindset as the world. You must be transformed.

Knowing that the Bible does not transform you, we need the power of God to transform us.

The transformation, we are to be changed into His image, into the reflection of Christ

Our constant prayer should be for the Lord to transform us, to set us free in our daily lives, to live for Him and not for the world.

20

The Bible

Creation

"In the beginning God created the heavens and the earth" (Gen. 1:1).

"By faith we understand that the worlds were framed by the Word of God, so that the things which are seen were not made of things which are visible" (Heb. 11:3).

"The Lord by wisdom founded the earth; by understanding He established the heavens; by His knowledge the depths were broken up and the clouds drop down the dew" (Proverbs 3:19–20).
"You Lord, in the beginning laid the foundation of the earth and the heavens are the work of Your hands" (Heb. 1:10).

"In the beginning was the Word, and the Word was with God and the Word was God. All things were made through Him and without Him nothing was made that was made" (John 1:1–2).

There was no big bang! God spoke.

Why Study the Bible?

"All Scripture is given by inspiration of God, and is profitable for doctrine, for reproof, for correction, for instruction in righteousness" (2 Timothy 3:16).

Because the Scripture is powerful and alive! It keeps us from sin and it helps us to gain a close relationship with the Lord. The kingdom of God is about growth.

The Word of God is alive.

Are you unable to sleep at night? Do not pick up that secular book! Pick up the Bible and see what the Lord wants to say to you.

The Bible is our user handbook on how we are to live our lives and serve our Lord. It is good to read at least a chapter everyday.

"The grass withers, the flower fades, but the word of our God stands forever" (Isa. 40:8).

"All flesh is as grass, and all the glory of man as the flower of the grass. The grass withers and its flower falls away, but the Word of the Lord endures forever" (1 Pet. 1:24–25).

Everything in the bible is a story to restore the habitation between God and man. We need to restore the fellowship between man and God.

"Man shall not live by bread alone; but man lives by every word that proceeds from the mouth of the Lord" (Deut. 8:4b).

How can we know the bible is true? Look at the history of Israel. Read the bible and compare it with Israel's history. You will find it totally amazing!

Remember: God's Word does not change; we are the ones who change.

For You

Why study our Bibles? It is our spiritual food.

"As newborn babes, desire the pure milk of the word, that you may grow thereby" (1 Pet. 2:2).

Do not deceive yourselves by reading the Word of God and not doing what it says.

Pay attention to the Scriptures when you study, live what you learn.

We have decisions to make everyday. We are to make good godly decisions; the only way we can is through studying the Word of God.

The Scriptures are our manual for living a life that is pleasing to the Lord. Do not just read the Word of God but live what you read and let it change your life so people will comment on the new you.

The Bible increases our faith and draws us closer to Him: "So then faith comes by hearing, and hearing by the word of God" (Rom. 10:17).

We must be faithful to the Word of God, obey the gospel, and live it.

Being in the word of God keeps us from sin. "Your word I have hidden in my heart, that I might not sin against You" (Ps. 119:11).

We must be faithful to the Word of God, obey the gospel and live it.

The moment we stop reading His Word is when we start losing sight of Him. He does not move from us, we move from Him.

Here is a quote from John Wesley: "Oh, give me that Book! At any price, give me the Book of God! Here is knowledge enough for me. Let me be a man of one Book."

We should all be with him on this one. There is only one book that matters. The only inspired book of God! Do not just read it; every word is for you too. Live what you read, learn and live it! The Lord will be glorified.

There are so many wolves in sheep's clothing; we must deprogram ourselves and get back into the truth of God's Word.

The Bible is our training manual for the correct way to run our life. Do not follow what man decided is correct; it can lead you to destruction. With the help of the Holy Spirit, you will understand what you are reading on your own.

Read and study the Bible. Pray always throughout the day and never take your eyes off of our risen Savior the Lord Jesus Christ. Let Him lead and guide you, not the world.

In the body of the Lord, there are too many that are not following Scripture! We accept and tolerate unholy alliances. This is not glorifying the Lord.

When you spend so much time around worldly people, you become like them. Get back into reading the Scriptures daily; you will be so much happier and at peace.

Does the Lord wake you up at night? Do not open up a romance novel or some other secular book. Pick up the Holy Scriptures and let God talk to you. Awesome!

"Whoever drinks of this water will thirst again, but whoever drinks of the water that I shall give him will never thirst. But the water that I shall give him will become in him a fountain of water springing up into everlasting life" (John 3:13–14).

Yes! The water Jesus is telling us about is the Word of God. Read it daily; learn it and live it! It does not get any better than this.

Be led by the Word of God, not by your feelings. Trust in Him.

The Word of God is "God-breathed." Anyone who tries to go against the Word of God (saying: God will understand) is living Satan's lie.

To get a close relationship with the Lord, we must get to know Him by reading His Word (the Bible) every day.

If your favorite Old Testament patriarch is Hercules, I think you need to do a little more Bible study.

There was a study that shows most crimes occur on Friday night. Just stay at home and build a relationship with Jesus. Study His Word and pray.

So many people ask: How do you know what God wants? Read His Word is how. The Lord will speak to you through His written Word.

We must hear and obey.

Did you know that life does have an instruction manual? It's called the Bible, basic instructions before leaving earth. Study to show yourself approved unto God.

"Be diligent to present yourself approved to God, a worker who does not need to be ashamed, rightly dividing the word of truth" (2 Tim. 2:15).

It is not enough to study the Word of God; we need to cling to Him and His Words in our daily life.

Our Lord looks for the person who not only hears His words, but also puts them into practice; to do what you hear is to have a good solid foundation.

Books written by man are usually far less than we expect, but the book of the Lord is full of surprises. It is a mass of light, a mountain of priceless revelations. Read the only inspirited Word of God.

To learn the purpose of life, get into the Word and study it daily. Cling to Him, ask Him: what do You have for me personally?

The Bible Deception

Remember, it is wrong to try to twist and turn the Word of God to please ourselves; that would be Satan's doing.

Do not follow anyone. Do not take to heart what man tells you about what is in the Bible. Look it up yourself and be your own person. We will be accountable before the Lord.

"But be doers of the Word, and not hearers only. Deceiving yourselves" (James 1:22).

Our Lord looks for the person who not only hears His Words but also puts them into practice. You may hear the Word of God and only increase your condemnation. But to do what you hear is to have a good foundation. There must be practical godliness, or nothing is right inside of us. The ones who "hear and do" have built a house with a stable foundation. This is the wisest, safest, and hardest thing to do.

Do not be like the unwise one who "would hear and ignore"; he would build his house upon the sand, and when a storm would come, it would sink.

People attack Genesis so much, because if you attack Genesis, then everything else is discredited. We must stand up for the Word of God!

Do not have a Bible study with teachers that are worldly. Satan will use them to make you not see the Word of God clearly! But to turn the words around to show you that sin is good and accepted by God! If you are in a sinful relationship because you have been shown the "twisted teachings" of Satan, go and seek a good, highly established

Baptist preacher and have him show you the truth in the Scripture.

The Lord tells us to lay aside all filthiness and overflow of wickedness, and receive with meekness the implanted Word of God, which is able to save your souls.

The first rule of Bible interpretation is when the plain sense makes sense, seek no other sense; otherwise you end up with nonsense!

How well do you know the Bible? Look at these verses. What do they tell you and where are they located?

> My God, My God, why have You forsaken Me? Why are You so far from helping Me, and from the words of My groaning? O My God, I cry in the daytime, but You do not hear; and in the night season, and am not silent. All those who see Me ridicule Me: They shoot out the lip, they shake the head, saying, He trusted in the LORD, let Him rescue Him; Let Him deliver Him, since He delights in Him! I am poured out like water and all My bones are out of joint: My heart is like wax; It has melted within Me, My strength is dried up like a potsherd, and My tongue clings to My jaws; You have brought Me to the dust of death. For dogs have surrounded Me; the congregation of the wicked has enclosed Me. They pierced My hands and My feet: I can count all My bones. They look and stare at Me. They divide My garments among them. And for My clothing they cast lots.

No, this is not in the New Testament; this is a prophecy from the Old Testament. This is in the book of Psalms at 22:1–2, 7–8, 14–18.

Read your Bible, learn it, and love the writings of our Lord.

Our Lord looks for the person who not only hears His words, but also puts them into practice. Hearing is not enough.

Then follow the Great Commission: "And He said to them. Go into all the world and preach the gospel to every creature" (Mark 16:15).

This is a command from Jesus. After we learn the Word of God, it is our responsibility to tell as many people as we can about the Gospel of the Lord. Tell them why you love Jesus so much, and what He has done for you.

21

The Church

"I was glad when they said to me, "Let us go into the house of the LORD" (Ps. 122:1).

Jesus had zeal for the house of God. We are to have the same zeal for our local church.

We are to love to go to the house of God, which is our local church.

Like David, we should be glad to go to church, to be filed with His Word, and to give worship to the Lord. We are to go to be a collective witness to the community that we love the Lord.

It is good to come together to proclaim God's praises. We need to take the time to be there for God. Some people think, okay, I went to church. I was there, the pastor did his job I gave some money, and I'm out of here. Then when they walk through those doors, they feel that they did their duty and God is happy as they continue walking down the road of destruction. Please do not let this be you!

We are to learn, we are to hunger for a close relationship with Jesus; we are to love Him more than we love ourselves. We are to turn our backs on the world and focus on pleasing Jesus with everything we say and do. We have a job to do—

the Great Commission is for all of us. The pastor's job is to equip us to serve the Lord, not to drag ourselves to the church once a week and say you did your duty.

When going to church, through the pastor's message, the lost are to become saved, the Christian is to become a warrior, and through the message the warrior's battle wounds are to be healed. We are to be totally equipped to leave the building and head back to the front lines of the battlefield to serve the Lord.

We need to step back on our everyday lives and worship the Lord with all of our hearts, and then we will get stronger in the Lord. Through the pastor's message, we will be equipped to serve.

Remember: going to church does not make you a Christian any more than going into a garage makes you a car. We must be a reflection of Christ. If we consider ourselves a Christian, we are to live our lives the way Jesus would live. We are to be His holy ambassadors. That is what it means to be a Christian.

Better is one day in the house of God than anywhere else.

Okay, we all had a wonderful uplift in church. Now, let us use what we learned during the service all week, never stop sharing what we learned.

When the offering plate is passed, we are to bring our offerings unto the Lord with great joy!

Be careful, if your Sunday religion is forgotten during the week, then it is a sham. You have mocked and insulted Christ in your hymns and prayers.

If your religion leads to sin, it is worse than no religion at all.

When you see that the Lord has brought one of His servants to you, do not ever turn down their help! Jesus brought them to you to build you up. We are to be zealous to build up the house of God. Does it devour you and consume you?

God wants His house to be filled with people zealous for Him.

We need to go to the house of the Lord regularly to be refreshed.

The church is more than a weekly chore! It should be a heart-moving experience as we open up our heart to God and let Him change us!

Do not just nonchalantly invite someone to the house of God; be excited about the services and insist that they come, persuade them. God wants His house full.

We are to get to know people, so we can help them in overcoming their objections to coming to the house of God.

One of the greatest freedoms we have in the United States is to be able to go to church, to learn, grow into a close relationship with, and to serve God. Do not take this freedom for granted.

22

Grow Close to the Lord

To grow close to the Lord, one needs to have a relationship with Him.

You can always tell a person that loves the Lord. You can see it in his character; he is a reflection of Christ with everything he says and does.

We must always beware of anything, which would damage that in you. We must let other things come and go in our lives. People will criticize you, but never allow anything to obscure the life that you have in Christ Jesus. Never let the world hurry you out of the relationship of abiding in Him. It is the one thing that is easy to fluctuate but it should not.

"When You said, 'Seek My face,' my heart said to You, 'Your face, Lord, I will seek'" (Ps. 27:8).

Like David, we are to also seek the face of the Lord. Ask the Holy Spirit for His help, and He will help you to seek the Lord's face. We need to hunger for a close relationship with the Lord.

You see your best friend everyday; you know what to say and what not to say. You get along so well that you want to be in their presence everyday. Jesus wants to be your best friend.

"Show me Your ways, O LORD; teach me Your paths. Lead me in Your truth and teach me, for You are the God of my salvation" (Ps. 25:4–5).

A good way to start is to search for the Lord.

"Ask and it will be given to you; seek and you will; find; knock and it will be opened to you. For everyone who asks receives and he who seeks finds and to him who knocks it will be opened" (Matt. 7:7–8).

We need a zeal for having a relationship, closeness with God.

We need to strive to know the Lord personally; we are to have a great passion for Him and to be hungry for a closer relationship with Him. We are to strive to get more of God everyday.

We need to pray and to study the Word of God and to live what we read. Not just a day here and a day there, but every day. We need to fall in love with Jesus, and you will not want to stop talking about Him.

I have people asking me all the time, how am I able to get closer to the Lord? My answer is simple. Turn off the secular music, stop going to secular concerts, and throw away your worldly books. If the music is not glorifying the Lord, then you should not be listening to it. If God does not inspire the book you are reading, then you should not be reading it. Anything else will only keep you from that close relationship with the Lord you are seeking.

Glorify the Lord with everything you do and say.

Do you feel far away from God? The Lord says to us in scripture: "Draw near to God and He will draw near to you" (James 4:8a).

No one should be more important to you than Jesus. Make sure you do not brag about anyone more than you brag about Him.

We are to spend time with the Lord not only every day but throughout the day. You will be amazed how close of a relationship you will start to build with the Lord. We must get rid of the idols in our lives and focus solely upon the Lord.

As King David always meditated upon the Lord all day and night, we should also learn from him. We are to keep in constant meditation with our Lord.

"I will meditate on the glorious splendor of Your majesty and on Your wondrous works" (Ps. 145:5).

Let us get into fellowship with Christ, give ourselves to Him without reserve.

We cannot handle what life brings to us alone. We need help; we need a personal relationship with Jesus the Messiah.

We are to strive for a continuous close relationship with the Lord. My book, *Encouragement*, can help! Check it out it will really help you to gain the relationship you are seeking to have with the Lord.

Knowing about the Lord does not mean that you know the Lord. You know about the president, but you really do not know him. We must get to really know the Lord.

Let Jesus be the one you would run to in good times as well as in bad times. Let Him give you the comfort that is beyond all understanding that can only come from God.

Do not yoke yourself together with unbelievers. Remember, one bad apple turns the entire basket bad.

It is not easy serving the Lord. Your old worldly friends will not like you. But, it is okay. Jesus offers you eternal life; they cannot.

Your friends want to go someplace; you know it is not the place for you to be. It is wrong, listen to the Holy Spirit, and do not go!

To grow close to the Lord: The Lord's will has to increase in our lives, while our will has to decrease.

Who is your best friend? Who do you run to in times of trouble? Let it be Jesus, only Jesus.

If you are in the workplace, you do not work for the "man," you are to work very hard to glorify Jesus through your work. You have one boss—the Lord Jesus Christ—you work for Him. Since you work to bring Jesus honor and glory, you will be the best employee in the workplace.

The Lord wants you to be a new person in Christ Jesus, to throw away the old sinful man and to be a new person in Christ Jesus.

If we really want to grow in the Lord, He must increase in our lives and we must decrease. Do not live for yourself, live to bring honor and glory to Him. Let the Lord be the passion of our desire.

"For whoever does the will of My Father in heaven is My brother and sister and mother" (Matt. 12:50).

Expect the Lord to move in your life and He will move!

Like a seed has to die in order to produce, we are to die to ourselves (to our old nature) to become a new creation for the Lord to use us to further His kingdom.

23

The Way of the Christian

If we consider ourselves Christians, we are to keep on striving for a personal relationship with Jesus where we will understand His call for us. Then we will do things out of sheer love for Him on our own account.

The way of the Christian, the real Christian, is to talk of God's wondrous works in your life. Tell me the old, old story. Tell it simply, as to a little child. More glory will come to God from that, more comfort to your soul in reflection and more benefit to the souls of those you teach.

We are all part of the Great Commission. We all have a job to do for the Lord.

"And the disciples were first called Christians in Antioch" (Acts 11:26b).

Please take notice: the disciples, that would be the eleven disciples that were with Jesus along with the other servants, were called Christians! If we consider ourselves Christians, then we must serve the Lord like His disciples did!

Do you hear the Lord calling out to you? Just say, "Here I am Lord," and let Him use you and let go of your own will. Give Him your life. Is He calling out to you. Do not tune

Him out, say, "Yes, Lord! Here I am. I belong to You, use me to bring You glory."

Being a Christian requires so much more than just going to church on Sundays. True followers of the Lord are to be His ambassadors, to be used by Him to further His kingdom.

We have to stop playing "Bible study"; we now have to live what we have learned throughout the years. If we keep what we have learned to ourselves, how is that glorifying the Lord?

Go out into the world and tell everyone you see what Jesus means to you, and why you love Him so much. Capture the heart of Jesus with your service for Him this coming week.

Being a follower of Jesus is not a Sunday-only thing. It is a way of life. We are ambassadors for the King of kings and the Lord of lords!

Our loyalty to Jesus should be seen and heard in our daily lives. That is what it means to be a Christian.

Going through our everyday lives, we cannot stop talking about what we are doing in our lives (the football game, the weather, the spouse, the children).

We as Christians need to put ourselves on the back burner and Jesus on the front burner. We need to talk about Jesus more than we talk about ourselves. He needs to be first in our lives.

Always remember: Christianity is not a religion; it is a relationship with the Lord Jesus Christ.

A good rule of thumb: do not go where Jesus would not go. Do not say what Jesus would not say. We are to be His reflection if we belong to Him.

You can build your life upon what pleases you, upon the sand of worldliness, which will sink. Or you can build your life upon the rock, the firm foundation of the risen Savior, of the Lord Jesus Christ.

Are you working for fame? Do you strive to obtain a great name? Those ambitions are very exhausting. Those who reach the top will find it very lonely and a very unsteady place. We are not to care for man's praise; it is like the wind in the air. If you want to rise to a great name, become a follower of Jesus, for the name of Christ is the name above every other name. Christ will not make you great among men, but He will make you small and very humble. He will give you rest from all of your dreams of worldly ambition but set a fire within you with a higher ambition than ever!

Our prayer should be: God give me the wisdom, discernment, and understanding to follow your footsteps.

We must get serious about our spiritual life now—tomorrow may be too late.

We must acquire an appetite for biblical truth, a deeper hunger to read the Word of God and to live what we read.

Do not look back to your past. Jesus tells us to just look forward and follow Him.

We were all born with a purpose, with a mission from the Lord. You must ask the Lord what your mission is and serve Him with everything you have; that is what it means to be a Christian.

Our Lord looks for the person who not only hears His Words, but also puts them into practice. Hearing is not enough. You may hear the Word of the Lord and only increase your condemnation. You must put into practice what you learn.

We must strive to have practical godliness, or nothing is right inside of us.

People that follow Jesus are not to use their lives on earth for their own pleasure; they should spend their lives serving the Lord and others. You will be greatly blessed.

Remember the parable of the man who built his house upon the rock and the other one who build his house upon the sand? We must be the one who had the solid foundation of the Lord.

"I will instruct you and teach you in the way you should go; I will guide you with My eye. Do not be like the horse or like the mule, which have no understanding which must be harnessed with bit and bridle" (Ps. 8–9a).

The Lord wants to lead and to guide us throughout our lives. Let Him instruct you and teach you the way you are to go, we are to stop trying to lead our own life. Remember, the Lord looks for the person who not only hears His words but also puts them into practice.

The true Christian is not the person who has only good words on their tongue, but the one who has God's will on their heart and in their life. There must be holiness in us, for without holiness, no one will see the Lord through you.

Christians must be doers of the Word, not remain in the dark.

"But be doers of the Word not hears only, deceiving yourselves" (James 1:22).

"If anyone loves Me, he will keep My Word" (John 14:23a).

We must apply the Word to our lives.

Do not be afraid. We have the Holy Spirit, and we are to be at total peace. We will overcome. The Christian is to have the light of peace in our lives. Do not waste your life in darkness. We are to cling to Him more than clinging to our own lives!

"He who loves his life will lose it and he who hates his life in this world will keep it for eternal life" (John 12:25).

The Lord says, "They will know you by your fruits."

You love the Lord and serve Him, but you have another side. I have so much fun with unsaved friends. I'm sure the Lord understands. No! The Lord does not understand. This person is walking on a fence. The Lord wants all of us, not just part time servants. The Lord wants *all* of us.

"But as for me I would seek God" (Job 5:8a).

No matter what we are going through, no matter how hard the situation is, never stop seeking God.

Jesus loves you, seek Him, and you will find Him. Then cling to Him and never let go! He wants you to be His ambassador. Just say yes Lord!

God has a plan; He will restore you. Wait upon the Lord.

Christianity is not just memorizing and repeating certain verses; it is yielding the heart and the life to Christ.

We are not under the law. Christ took us from bondage of a condemning covenant and made us to receive the adoption of children so we can cry, Abba, Father.

We as Christians need to live by the Lord's rules. We have to be changed from the inside out. Are you a reflection of Christ? This should be the Christian's goal if we really belong to Him.

Christians do not simply believe in Christ or imitate Christ from a distance. We have been united to Jesus Christ by the power of the Spirit. We are united to Christ as branches are united to the vine. We are in Christ.

"I am the vine, you are the branches. He who abides in Me and I in him bears much fruit" (John 14:5a).

Let us, who call ourselves Christians, remember that we are not to lift up doctrine, the church, or our denomination. The Son of Man must be lifted up!

As Christians, we believe that we are born twice. We have received a new and heavenly life. My question is: what do we do more than others?

We should show that there is more in us than in others by letting more of Jesus come out of us. If we truly believe in

Jesus, much more is expected of us than of the ones that are not "reborn spiritually." If the professed Christian is no better in his daily conversation, then the ungodly depend upon it, he is no Christian. We possess a higher life; we are lifted to a higher platform than the worldly man. We must lead a nobler life and be guided by the highest moral spiritual value. Let the children of darkness meet evil with evil and carry on their wars, fighting, lying, backbiting, as well as their revenge. But for us, we are believers, we are the children of the God of love and we must serve the Lord with everything we say and do.

All Christians should be heavenly minded, keeping our eyes off of worldliness and constantly upon heaven, upon Jesus. He will help us to overcome the world!

A true Christian lives his life as if running a race with Jesus our Lord at the finish line. Many people think they are a believer but do not know the Lord.

"Not everyone who says to Me Lord, Lord, shall enter the kingdom of heaven, but he who does the will of My Father in heaven" (Matt. 7:21).

"And then I will declare to them, I never knew you; depart from Me, you who practice lawlessness!" (Matt. 7:23).

Anyone can say that they are a Christian, but can we say that we are His disciples?

Christianity should not be our religion; it should be our lifestyle.

24

Following the Lord

Jesus tells us to turn our back on our past and to follow Him. Jesus tells us "not to look back" on our past. Just look straight ahead and follow Him. "Another disciple said to Him, Lord, first let me go and bury my father." But Jesus told him, Follow Me and let the dead bury their own dead" (Matt. 8:21–22).

We must let go of our past, stop looking back and set our sights only on our future, and let Jesus lead your life.

You like the world but still want to please the Lord—Jesus says that He will not tolerate this. He wants all of you.

"So then because you are lukewarm, neither cold nor hot, I will vomit you out of My mouth" (Rev. 3:16).

He does not take pleasure in lukewarm followers. In following the Lord, there is not any middle ground; there is not any gray. The Lord needs 100 percent of you.

Following the Lord will cost you something. Are you ready to pay the price?

There are so many Christians that want to follow the Lord, but things or our own wants always get in the way. The

Lord will bring you to the place where He would ask you to give your all for Him, and then we will begin to debate.

The Lord just might produce a crisis where we have to decide…to live for the Lord or against the Lord's leading and from that point the great divide begins. If the crisis has come your way, you must surrender your will to Him fully.

Do not be ashamed to be called narrow-minded. During life's journey, if you are on the right road, you will find the gate somewhat difficult and very narrow; it demands self-denial and strict obedience.

There is another road which so many like to go down, the road of the world, but it leads to destruction. People go to ruin along the freeway of this road, but the way to heaven is very narrow. Always remember: do not follow the crowd, they can be wrong; only follow Jesus.

The big question is: did you give up all worldliness to follow the Lord? Does everything you do and everywhere you go glorify the Lord?

All Christians should be heavenly minded, keeping our eyes off of the world and constantly upon heaven, upon Jesus.

We as followers of Jesus, have a high calling. We are His ambassadors.

"I will instruct you and teach you in the way you should go; I will guide you with My eye" (Ps. 32:8). How awesome is this!

If you give your all to the Lord, He will lead and guide you in your life and He will be glorified through you.

We must follow the Lord and stay in the center of His will. Never take your eyes off the risen Savior, the Lord Jesus Christ. We cannot make it without Him. Praise Him!

God the Father told Jesus to lay down His life; we also are to lay down our life for the Lord. Do not just sit there and blend in with everyone else! Share your passion for Jesus, tell as many people as you can why you love Him so much.

Remember, your life does not belong to you anymore because you have been bought with a price. To act like your life is yours will never work. If you associate with an unbeliever, just make sure it is you who are affecting them and they are not affecting you. Do not yoke yourself together with unbelievers.

If you are God's child, your future is not in your hands, but in the capable hands of your sovereign Savior of wisdom, power, and might.

"If anyone desires to come after Me, let him deny himself and take up his cross and follow Me" (Matt. 16:24).

Yes, that is what it means to follow the Lord. We must deny ourselves and follow, serve the Lord. The Lord has given all of us a special talent; what is your talent? Are you using it to glorify the Lord? In a man's heart, a man plans his course, but the Lord determines his steps.

Being His disciples means saying no to ourselves. Are we submitted to His plan? Dying to sin, to selfishness, saying no to yourself? If we belong to Him we are to be changed from the inside out. We must bear good fruit for all to see. We are His ambassadors.

Do you walk in the light of the Lord through Scripture? Ask the Lord to help us not to turn away from that light; instead, we should feel that it is our friend and we should feel the deep desire to walk in it and follow the Lord. Those who seek the light will find it.

It should be our constant goal to belong to Him.

We need to look for satisfaction in Christ Jesus.

We need to be filled with the fullness of God.

Immerse yourself in Jesus. We need to grow in Him, talk to Him throughout the day and fall in love with Jesus more and more.

Jesus gave His all for you, what are you giving Him in return?

Jesus did not die so we could keep on living for ourselves. He died so we could live for Him.

Jesus must become greater in our lives while we become less.

As followers of Jesus, we each have a ministry. Ask the Lord to lead you to yours.

The plans Jesus has for you are not the same plans you have for yourself. Follow the Lord, and you will be blessed.

Jesus tells us to not look back on our past lives, just keep on following Him. You will be greatly blessed.

When someone would come up against you today, shower them with love. Be a reflection of Jesus to them; love them like Jesus would.

To be a follower of Jesus, we must decrease while the Lord must increase in our lives. We are not to live for ourselves; we are to live to serve the Lord.

How do we get to know the Lord? You know His character by reading His Word from back to back. A prayer relationship with God is very important. Ask the Holy Spirit to help—He will.

A true Christian does not just hear the Word of God, but he is also a doer; he does what the Word of God says. The Bible is for you and for me; we are to love and live what we read in the Lord's Holy Word. We must follow and serve.

Do not ever go where Jesus would not go. Do not ever say what Jesus would not say. Do not defile your body for if you belong to Jesus, your body is the temple of the Holy Spirit. To belong to Jesus we must be a reflection of Him.

To have a close relationship with the Lord, a good guide would be to have a daily:

1. prayer and worship time;
2. Scripture and Bible study to energize your life;
3. personal, quiet one-on-one time with the Lord.

You then would be amazed at the closeness you would have with the Almighty God. Keep your eyes focused only upon the Lord today! Let Him be glorified with everything you do and say. Bless Him at all times in good times as well as in bad times.

You must let go of the past and live for the future. Keep your eyes upon the Lord and never look back. To believe in Him, to love Him with all your heart, and to obey His leading just as Noah and his family obeyed. That is what the Lord wants from all of us. Not just Noah and his family, you and me also. When Satan tells you to forget about the Lord and live your own life to please yourself; turn your back on him and he will flee from you and follow the Lord. You will be blessed.

When you are old and sickly you do not want to regret your life outside of the Lord. Make a total commitment and live for Him now!

25

Whose Side Are We On?

We are either for Jesus or against Him.

"He who is not with Me is against Me" (Matt. 12:30a).

There is no other way!

"He who says, I know Him and does not keep His commandments, is a liar and the truth is not in him. But whoever keeps His Word, truly the love of God is perfected in him. By this we know that we are in Him" (1 John 2:4).

We are either for Jesus or we are against Him; you either live in the world or you live to serve Jesus, there is not any in-between.

We are called to be a son of God. Do not run from the Lord; run to the Lord!

The moment we stop reading His word is when we start losing sight of Him. He does not move from us, we move from Him. Choose to make it a habit in your daily life to read His Word and to live it everyday.

Are we living our lives to please ourselves, or are we living our lives for Jesus, to further His kingdom? Live your life for Jesus, and He promises you eternal life with Him forever.

In the book of Romans, one of my many favorite books in the Bible, the Lord, through Paul, tells his people back then and us today: "Therefore God gave them over in the sinful desires of their hearts to sexual impurity for the degrading of their bodies with one another. They exchanged the truth of God for a lie" (Rom. 1:24).

We are to be holy and pure in our lives. Do not let the world pull you down and away from God. Do no let society get you to exchange the truth of God for a lie. Read your Bible everyday and attend a good Bible-preaching church so you can be strong in the Lord and know what God expects from His children and to please the Creator of all things, our Lord and Savior Jesus Christ.

We are all on a journey in life. We have a choice as to which road to go down. Jesus is calling...

To live for Jesus, we must bury our own will and live for Him. Choose Him.

Remember Noah's Ark? Don't wait until tomorrow to come to Jesus, tomorrow might be too late.... do not miss the boat!

26

Are We Living for Christ?

The Lord's will has to increase in our lives while our will has to decrease.

Remember, if you really belong to Jesus; His best friends were His apostles, not worldly friends. One bad apple can turn the entire bunch bad.

Do not let anyone lead you astray.

Be careful who you let enter our inner circle…bad company corrupts good character.

Blessed is he who takes refuge in Him.

Whom does your heart belong too? Let it belong to Christ.

We are not here to get the approval of men…but of God.

What does the Lord want from us? We are to consecrate ourselves unto the Lord. Hunger for God's Word and live our lives to please Him.

Let us be a reflection of Jesus today, let your friends, coworkers and family want and hunger for what they see in you, Jesus.

Do not become like the world. Live for Jesus.

People are so concerned about pleasing others that they end up neglecting Jesus. People pleasing will not get you to heaven.

Are we living our lives for ourselves, or are we living our lives for Jesus, to be used by Him to further His kingdom.

Follow Jesus, do not look back. Your commitment is not there. Look straight ahead, like running a race with Jesus at the finish line.

The difference between the true child of God and the person who claims to be a Christian cannot be seen with the naked eye, but the Lord sees it.

Watch your circle of friends. If all your friends speak Italian, eventually you will start to speak it too.

We must examine ourselves, are we happy with what we see? Look at life, our life from God's perspective. The world we live in is immoral. Things we accept are immoral in God's sight. We must not be of the world if we are living for Christ.

The source of American values went from the church to Hollywood. Compare the *Leave It to Beaver* to the *Family Guy*.

We need discipline. Remove images that are not edifying you, that are not bringing you closer to God. Replace the media with Christian music and God's Word. Separate yourselves from unbelievers or people who do not serve Christ; they will only bring you down.

Are we living according to our old nature? Or do we have a new life in Christ Jesus. You can say: yes, I do have a new life in Jesus! My question is: how many people have commended on the drastic change in you? If people have seen and commended on the wonderful change, then praise the Lord! If no one has said a word about the change, then the old man is still there. Ask the Lord to help you to really make that change.

> "You will know them by their fruits. Do men gather grapes from thorn bushes or figs from thistles? Even so, every good tree bears good fruit, but a bad tree bears bad fruit. A good tree cannot bear bad fruit. A good tree cannot bear bad fruit, nor can a bad tree bear good fruit. Every tree that does not bear good fruit is cut down and thrown into the fire. Therefore by their fruits you will know them." (Matt. 7:16–20)

Look at how you are living your life. Do people see you bearing good fruit for the Lord, or are you bearing bad sinful fruit?

When we are living for Christ, your old friends will start to keep a distance from you. You will not want to go to the same places as you used to. You will have a deep hunger to be holy. For the Lord tells us to be holy, for He is holy. Remember, people will classify you by the company you keep. Be careful not to be seen with the wrong types of people and in the wrong worldly places; it will bring your testimony down.

Let go of your life and let Jesus lead you. Let Jesus guide you down the road; He has created for you to go down to serve Him.

The Lord did not create you to be placed upon this earth just to have a good time and to live for ourselves. We were given a choice: to live for ourselves or to live for the Lord. The Lord promises us eternal life with Him.

The big question is: did you give up all worldliness to follow the Lord? Does everything you do and everywhere you go glorify Him?

"He has shown you, O man, what is good; and what does the LORD require of you. But to do justly, to love mercy and to walk humbly with your God" (Mic. 6:8).

"For I am the LORD your God. You shall therefore consecrate yourselves and you shall be holy; for I am holy" (Lev. 11:44a).

Jesus is Lord!

Let us seek to know the Lord's mind, to learn the Lord's will, to study the Lord's book, and to receive the Lord's Spirit. We are to make disciples throughout the nations; we are to do His work and not our own. That is what it means to be living for Christ.

Let us who call ourselves Christians remember that we are not to lift up doctrine, the church, or our denomination. The Son of Man must be lifted up!

Never stop falling in love with Jesus. Live everyday as His ambassadors.

Take a step back and look at your life. Are you doing your will or the will of the Lord? Be very careful. Doing the will of the Lord is "not living in the world, but living for the kingdom of the Lord."

"If we endure, we shall also reign with Him. If we deny Him, He also will deny us" (2 Timothy 2:12a).

Be careful. Die with Him; live with Him, reign with Him. It does not get any simpler than that. Living in the world is denying the Lord; do not let this happen to you.

Christians do not simply believe in Christ or imitate Christ from a distance. We have been united to Jesus Christ by the power of the Spirit. We are united to Christ as branches are united to the vine. We are in Christ. As Jesus tells us: "Abide in Me and I in you. As the branch cannot bear fruit of itself, unless it abides in the vine, neither can you, unless you abide in Me I am the vine, you are the branches. He who abides in Me and I in him, bears much fruit; for without Me you can do nothing" (John 15:4–5).

Every true child of God glorifies Christ. If you cannot say you are glorifying Christ, you should question whether you really belong to Him. If you are His, this is true of you. We glorify Christ by our patient suffering, our bold witness, and our efforts to extend His kingdom, by our Christian virtues and our faith in Him.

"Crucify him!"

That is what the Jews shouted when Pilate asked what crime has Jesus committed. Of course, we know that Jesus did not commit any crime. Pilate thought that by having Jesus flogged, he could let him go. Flogging was the most terrible of tortures. Many died under it. It reduced the human body to a mass of bruised, bleeding flesh. This flogging produced the wounds by which we have been healed. For Christ, it was only the beginning of the awful end. Pilate knew Jesus was innocent of any crime. He even spoke out for Christ, but he did not help Him like he should have.

Are we following the footsteps of Pilate? Do we speak out for Jesus? Do we lack moral courage? Some would sooner be damned than be laughed at. Do not let this be you. Do not mock the Lord with empty praise and worship or Bible study. Do not glorify Satan by turning your back on Jesus like Pilate did.

"Who Himself bore our sins in His own body on the tree, that we, having died to sins, might live for righteousness, by whose stripes you were healed" (1 Pet. 2:24).

Jesus is Lord!

Let us seek to know the Lord's mind, to learn the Lord's will, to study the Lord's book, and to receive the Lord's Spirit. We are to make disciples throughout the nations; we are to do His work and not our own.

Rejoice in the Lord always. Again I say, rejoice!

We must stay away from worldliness and be totally engulfed in the Lord.

Let go and let Jesus take over.

When we think about all of the pain and suffering Jesus went through for us, He is so worthy of our service for Him. He is worthy of our all.

Never let a day go by without being a witness for our Lord. This should be number one on your mind at all times.

Is the Lord tugging at your heart? Are you afraid to go into unchartered waters? The Lord wants to use you; just say, "Yes Lord!" and go!

The Lord is glorified when we go outside of our comfort zone to serve Him.

Submit your life unto the Lord and let Him lead and guide you down the road He has planned for you.

Be strong in the Lord.

We are to become less; Jesus is to become more in our lives.

Did Isaiah prophecy about you, saying, "Hypocrites! These people draw near to me with their mouth, and honor Me with their lips. But their heart is far from Me. And in vain they worship Me. Teaching as doctrines the commands of men" (Matt. 15:8–9).

Anyone can say that they love the Lord, the question is: does their lives show it?

Be careful that your god is not money, material things, or family. None of those can take away your sins or promise you eternal life.

Be careful of the one who is a hypocrite! He pretends to be a servant of God when all along he was a slave of Satan, serving his own self and sin.

We must be separate from the world while still living in the world.

Do not let friends or coworkers get you down. Stand firmly upon the solid rock of Jesus! Whatever you are going through, be His reflection.

Worship the Lord your God and serve Him only. Make sure you are serving Him in the workplace and with everything you do. Let people see Him in you.

When going to work and trying to be a witness for our Lord, do not go and play Sunday school teacher or preacher. Go and be yourself; let them see Jesus in and through you.

27

Serving the Lord

We must let our light shine.

Let our light shine for the Lord today. Do not hold back; holding back will only glorify Satan.

If we are followers of Christ, then we are to serve Him. We are a light in the darkness; let your light shine, to be used by the Lord to further his kingdom!

Let Jesus be the Alpha and Omega, the beginning and the end of your trust, your love and your witness for the Lord. Is there anything else worth telling lost people about?

If people do not see things in the right light, they may live in sin and yet think they are doing right. We should live up to our light, but if that light is itself darkness, what a mistake our whole lives will be!

If the world does not see any evidence that we truly believe what we claim to believe about God why would they want it? We must all let our light of our belief in Jesus the Messiah shine, shine, shine!

Our loyalty to Jesus should be seen and heard in our lives.

Jesus died for you, would you live for Him?

We are to be a reflection of Jesus. When they see the Lord in us, they will want what they see.

Be a light in the darkness; Jesus is depending on us!

If you love the Lord, do not hide your light under a basket! Let it shine. Let it shine for the honor and glory of the Lord!

If we walk in the light as He is in the light, we have fellowship with one another and the blood of Jesus Christ His Son cleanses us from all sin.

This world is so dark; we must be the light of the world. Let Jesus shine through you.

We are in Christ, when we witness we are speaking before God with sincerity, like men sent from God. We are sent from God to serve Him.

The wrath of God will be brought upon this world; God will protect His loyal servants.

Do not ever doubt your standing with God, if you know you are real with Him that is all that matters.

Let us be bold today and serve the Lord with all of our hearts like never before; let us bring Him honor and glory in the workplace today.

We have to get our minds renewed, away from the world, and set on serving the Lord.

Stop leading your own life. The Lord has a divine plan for you. Let Him take over, and you will be greatly blessed.

"But it is written: 'Eye has not seen, nor ear heard, nor have entered into the heart of man the things which God has prepared for those who love Him'" (1 Cor. 2:9).

To know the Lord and to make Him known to others should be our mission statement.

"If anyone serves Me, let him follow Me and where I am, there My servant will be also. If anyone serves Me, him My Father will honor" (John 12:26).

A man does not win souls to Christ while he is himself half asleep. The battle that is to be fought for the Lord Jesus must be fought by men/women who are wide-awake.

"And Jabez called on the God of Israel saying, 'Oh that You would bless me indeed, and enlarge my territory, that Your hand would be with me, and that You would keep me from evil, that I may not cause pain!' So God granted him what he requested" (1 Chron. 4:10).

Jabez was a man who hungered to do something for the Lord. He knew how to request something that His Lord wanted him to have. He did this because he was an honorable man with whom the Lord was pleased. It is all-important that we always choose what our Lord has already chosen for us. He already has our path made; all we must do is find it and follow it. He wanted to have the influence to be able to do something big for the Lord. We should have a great passion to do the same.

Note what he did for the Lord. He was not a self-seeker. He wanted God to receive the glory. He wanted to be the "instrument" God would use. I believe there is no greater calling than to be an instrument that God can use.

Note that Jabez wanted the Lord to be with him. "Let your hand be with me." He knew he could do nothing without God's presence.

One thing more, he wanted the Lord to keep him from harm and free from pain. We must take care what we do with our body. We must want to give our Lord a strong body so that there will be no impediment that would hinder our work for the Lord.

Just as Jabez was knocking upon the Lord's door and asking the Lord to expand his territory of service for him. We too must follow his lead.

You may want to serve the Lord, but do not know how? My first book, *Encouragement*, can be a big help!

Jesus died for you…would you live to serve Him?

"I will instruct you and teach you in the way you should go; I will guide you with My eye" (Ps. 32:8).

Yes, He will lead and guide you down the road that He wants you to go down to serve Him. Do not try to serve Him the way you want to serve, but run through the door that He has opened for you. The way we want to serve Him might not be what the Lord has planed for you.

Serve Him with all of your heart today, glorify Him greatly!

Even though people are against you, "be Christ to them." When you are serving the Lord, Satan will take notice. Stay strong and he will stay under your feet.

The circumstances of a saint's life are ordained of God. In the life of a saint, there is no such thing as chance. We show the world Jesus by letting Jesus shine through us.

Let Jesus be the Alpha and the Omega—the beginning and the end of your trust, your love, and your witness for the Lord. Is there anything else worth telling lost people about?

Serve the Lord with all of your heart today; make Jesus proud of you and your work for Him. Bless Him with your service. He is so worthy!

If you hear God's voice, do not harden your hearts. Say yes to the Lord and follow Him. Turn your back on the world and follow Jesus.

Yes, the Lord still speaks to us today. We need a close relationship with the Lord; read His Word and stay in prayer throughout the day.

Remember, tell everyone you see today about the love you have for the Lord, yes even the person who you cannot stand. You will be greatly blessed.

People are willing to pay a high price for something they value. Is it any surprise that Jesus would demand this much of a commitment from His followers?

People that follow Jesus are not to use their lives on earth for their own pleasure; they should spend their lives serving God and others.

We belong to Jesus. We are His ambassadors. Let us make Him proud of us today! How awesome to be used by the Lord to further His kingdom!

For the Son of Man will come in the glory of His Father with His angels, and He will reward each according to his works. Serve the Lord with all your heart!

"And behold, I am coming quickly and My reward is with Me to give to everyone according to his work" (Rev. 22:12).

We are all part of the Great Commission. We all have a job to do for the Lord.

Let your light shine for the Lord today. Do not hold back, holding back will only glorify Satan.

Let us serve the Lord with all our heart. Show the world whose side you are on. Praise the Lord.

Do not try to understand, just trust in the Lord with all of your heart. We can never understand the ways of the Lord; they are much too great!

As followers of Jesus, we each have a ministry. Ask the Lord to lead you to yours.

"Now the just shall live by faith: But if anyone draws back, My soul has no pleasure in him" (Heb. 10:38).

Never draw back from witnessing. We need to be like King David and capture the heart of the Lord with our services unto Him.

> Man's biggest need is to know the Lord
> The Lord wants us to know Him
> The Lord wants the world to know Him
> Do not be silent, witness!

Serving the Lord is our undeserved honor. Do not turn your back on being used as the Lord's tool to further His kingdom!

What an undeserving privilege it is for us, as small as we are to be able to serve the Creator of all things. To be used by the Almighty God. Wow!

We are not to be idle. If we belong to Jesus, we must serve Him. Be His ambassadors, His reflection wherever we go. This is what it means to belong to Christ.

Be strong, through our hardships the Lord will build us in character and draw us closer to Him. Never stop leaning upon the Lord.

As a servant of the Lord, our lives are in the hands of God like a bow and arrow in the hands of an archer. God is aiming at something we cannot see. Trust and go!

The heathen are perishing, and there is but one way of salvation for them, for there is but one name given under heaven among men whereby they must be saved.

The Lord says, "Whom shall I send?" If you will listen with the ear of faith, say, "Here I am, Lord, send me!" We are all to serve the Lord, not just some people; all of us are to serve Him if we really belong to Him.

"For I am the LORD your God. You shall therefore consecrate yourselves and you shall be holy; for I am holy" (Lev. 11:44a).

The Almighty God calls us to join an army that will bring the Gospel into the enemy territory. Go and follow the Lord's leading.

The plans Jesus has for you are not the same plans you have for yourself, follow the Lord's leading and you will be blessed.

Today is a day that the Lord has made! Let us serve the Lord with all of our heart, pray that the Lord will bring at least one person across your path to witness to today.

"Be doers of the Word, and not hearers only deceiving yourselves" (James 1:22).

We need to become a faithful servant. It takes an intimate relationship with God. Study His Word and write it in our hearts and serve Him. He will open doors in your life for you to be used by Him to further His Kingdom.

The easy way is not always the godly way.

We must have a close relationship with Jesus; we will be powerless without Him.

What is your talent? Are you asking the Lord to use that talent for His glory?

Be a servant that is ready and waiting. Be dressed and ready for action!

Sometimes the Lord will lead us outside of our comfort zone to serve Him. Be strong, the Lord is with you at all times. Never say, "No, Lord!"

Wherever God may lead us, if we do not know where we are going, at least we know with whom we are going. We do not know the road, but we know the guide. We must have faith and be strong to break through our comfort zone and go!

If you are in a ministry you do not like, who do you serve, yourself or the Lord? Let the Lord place you where He wants to use you! He has a plan for you if you live to serve Him.

Just like John the Baptist was busy until he was put into prison. He would not waste an hour while he had an opportunity to serve the Lord, and he did it with all of his heart. We must be like John! Spend every moment in the service of Christ while you can!

> And while they went to buy, the bridegroom came and those who were ready went in with him to the wedding; and the door was shut. Afterward the other virgins came also, saying, Lord, Lord, open to us! But he answered and said assuredly; I say to you, I do not know you. Watch therefore, for you know neither the day or the hour in which the Son of Man is coming. (Matt. 25:10–13)

We must be ready; the Lord will come when we do not expect Him. Those who are ready and waiting will be rewarded.

Be "bold" in serving our risen savior. If you are not bold and "draw back," the Lord will not be honored by you. Pray that the Holy Spirit of God will give you the boldness to proclaim the Lord to everyone you meet.

The Lord asks us to "set our affections on things above, not on things on the earth." How we serve and in what way we serve the Lord is up to the Lord, not us.

I was just thinking. When Jesus was carrying the cross, it did not take too long when the soldiers saw that when He was about to collapse, they saw a man from Cyrene called Simon and had him continue to carry the Lord's cross. Where was the other Simon, Simon Peter? Another man has taken his place. Simon lost the special blessing of helping the Lord. Do not let this happen to you! Sometimes the Lord's servants are negligent, and He finds other servants to take their place. I have seen this happen; it has happened to me one too many times. Stay true to Christ. Do not let another Simon take your place!

"Behold, I am coming quickly! Hold fast what you have, that no one may take your crown" (Rev. 3:11).

Simon Peter lost a crown here, and another Simon wore it.

Jesus loves you so much that He gave His life for you. All He wants from us is to be a vocal witness. Go and serve Him.

If you see the Lord has opened a door for you to go through to serve Him, do not hesitate! You must run through that door as fast as you can. The door will close quickly and you will lose your chance to serve the Lord.

We are to serve our Lord with all of our hearts. We each have a road to go down that the Lord has placed before us, just go!

Do we say: I want to move here or there to start my life? Or do we say: Lord lead me and guide me where You want to use me?

God calls us to join an army that will bring the Gospel into enemy territory. We must be equipped to go.

Serving the Lord is not just for pastors! They are to equip us to go out and serve our Lord. The Lord will not honor benchwarmers.

We must remember: the pastor's job is to equip us to go out into the world and witness for the kingdom of our Lord. He has his job, and we have ours. We are the Lord's ambassadors. Learn as much as you can from your pastor's teachings, then go out into the world and tell everyone you see what Jesus means to you and why you love Him so much. Capture the heart of Jesus with your service for Him this week.

The Lord has promised us a great inheritance. Be careful not to live for self, but in all we do, do it to glorify the Lord. We all have a race to run in our life here, Jesus is at the finish line. Let Him be proud of us in the way we lived our lives serving Him, turning our back on self and focusing on being His ambassadors.

"Knowing that from the Lord you will receive the reward of the inheritance; for you serve the Lord Christ" (Col. 3:24).

On Sunday, before going to the service, pray that the Lord will give you full understanding of what the He is telling you through the pastor so you can be equipped to serve the Him.

Be careful whom you bow your knee to. Will we serve the "gods" of this world or the God of creation? Will we serve the enticing distractions of contemporary life or the Holy One whose name is above all names?

Just say: yes, Lord, I want to give away my life to serve Jesus. Put aside your selfishness and live to serve the Lord, the Creator of all things, the one who died for you. He is so worthy.

So, you do not like where the Lord has placed you to serve Him? Well, your life belongs to Him. He wants you to learn, serve Him where you are, learn from the experience and wait for Him.

The big question: whom do you serve? Do you live to please the Lord with everything you do and say, or do you live in the world? You cannot do both.

"I know your works, that you are neither cold nor hot. I could wish you were cold or hot. So then, because you are lukewarm, and neither cold nor hot. I will vomit you out of My mouth" (Rev. 3:15).

Who do you love more than anyone? Do you love your spouse, child, maybe your pet more than words can tell? We should love the Lord more than anyone. To please Him should be our ambition, our passion.

We need His strength, understanding, wisdom, and knowledge. Then we need to server our Lord.

Is the Lord calling to you? As with Saul, the Lord told him to stop kicking against the goads. Stop refusing to open the door. Just say yes to the Lord!

If you serve the Lord, it's okay if you do not understand what is going on. Just keep your eyes on the Lord and never look back!

What does the Lord require of us?

- "He has shown you, O man what is good; and what does the LORD require of you. But to do justly, to Love mercy and to walk humbly with your God" (Mic. 6:8).
- "For I am the LORD your God. You shall therefore consecrate yourselves and you shall be holy; for I am holy" (Lev. 11:44a).

Our old nature is rotted by the world; we must strip off the old nature and become anew for the Lord.

Do you think so badly of the Lord as to think that He will give into your passions by giving you liberty to live in sin and yet go to heaven?

Your desires must be perfect. You must, from your heart, put away every single sin, be it of what shape it may, however pleasurable or painful it may appear. The Lord tells us: if our eyes cause us to sin, then pluck it out. It is better for you to enter into life maimed and blind than that you should perish in your transgressions.

We all have a race to run for our Lord. Let us run it as fast as we can with victory in our sights. To give Jesus full honor and glory

"'Whom shall I send, and who will go for Us?' Then I said, 'Here am I! Send me'" (Isa. 6:8).

God did not address the call to Isaiah; Isaiah overheard God saying, "Who will go for us?" The call of God is not for the special few, it is for everyone. The special ones are those who have come into a relationship with God through Jesus Christ. These are the ones like Isaiah. These are the ones who call out to God. Let there be a turning point in your life. Ask the Holy Spirit to lead you into a close relationship with Jesus through studying the Word of God and through prayer, then say, "Lord use me!"

The Lord has a plan for every one of us. We must search and pray to see that plan and then run through that door the Lord has open.

There are some of us that are radical for certain causes. Those causes are here by day and gone by night. Those causes will promise you nothing. Focus those radical tendencies toward serving Christ. You can put into good use all those bottled-up radical tendencies; use them to further the kingdom of God, use it to capture the heart of Jesus. There is a great promise when focusing your ambitions upon Christ, eternal life with Him and salvation of your loved ones forever. Stop wasting your radical tendencies; they will just go up in smoke, a vapor for nothing. Be radical for Jesus, and you will be greatly blessed.

We all have a job to do for the God of all creation. "But none of these things move me; nor do I count my life dear to myself, so that I may finish my race with joy and the ministry which I received from the Lord Jesus, to testify to the gospel of the grace of God" (Acts 20:24).

28

Be a Witness

We all have a job to do for the Lord. Do not let Satan hold you back. Witness with all your heart.

Serving the Lord is not just for pastors! They are to equip us to go out and serve our Lord. The Lord will not honor benchwarmers.

We must have a close relationship with Jesus; we will be powerless without Him.

Remember, tell everyone about the love you have for the Lord, yes, even the person who you cannot stand. You will be greatly blessed.

We need to live for God, to trust Him. Do not say that if this and what if that, then you are *not* trusting God. You need to be radical for Him

When we follow and serve Jesus, we may get the attention of Satan. He will get angry and start to attack us. We are to tell Satan to get out of the way! We serve the Almighty God.

We must witness with boldness, stand firm upon the solid rock of our savior Jesus the Christ. He is our refuge and salvation.

How many of us can say: for I am not ashamed of the Gospel of Jesus Christ? Then why are you not telling the world about Jesus?

We are not to be idle; if we belong to Jesus, we must serve Him. We must be His ambassadors, His reflection wherever we go. This is what it means to belong to Christ.

"Now the just shall live by faith: but if anyone draws back, My soul has no pleasure in him" (Heb. 10:38).

Never draw back from witnessing for the Lord!

Man's biggest need is to know the Lord; the Lord wants us to know Him. The Lord wants the world to know Him. Do not be silent, witness!

Satan will try as hard as he can to stop you from being a witness for the Lord. Do not give him the glory! Turn your back on him and he will flee.

Jesus tells us that if we do not tell people about Him, then He will not tell the Father in heaven about us. We must be a witness for our Lord.

"For whoever is ashamed of Me and My words in this adulterous and sinful generation, of him the Son of Man also will be ashamed when He comes in the glory of His Father with the holy angels" (Mark 8:38).

Do not let this happen to you! Witness for our Lord.

Today is a day that the Lord has made; let us serve the Lord with all of our heart! Let us be used by Him to further His kingdom!

Remember, the one person you decided not to witness to today might die tonight, lost in his sins without Jesus. Witness to everyone today.

You will not glorify God much unless you put your strength into the ways of the Lord and throw your body, soul, and spirit, your entire life into the work of the Lord.

If we leave Jesus out of our witness, we leave the son out of the day, the moon out of the night, the waters out of the ocean. There is no gospel worth proclaiming if Jesus is forgotten.

Witnessing is so important, so many people just do not understand. I'm telling you, do not be afraid to tell as many people as you can everyday why you love Jesus so much. We are to be the reflection of Jesus we are His ambassadors.

Pray every morning and ask the Lord to bring at least one person to you to witness to today.

Take advantage of any opportunity to be a witness unto the Lord.

Thank the Lord for the rain, even though it seems too much at times. Thank the Lord for the sunshine even though ninety degrees seems sweltering. Thank the Lord for giving us the wellness to get up and out of bed this morning. Thank Him in good times as well as in bad times. Tell everyone you see today why you love Him so much. Bring glory and honor to Jesus today.

Be a witness, do not keep Jesus to yourself and do not be afraid to be the witness the Lord wants you to be.

Never assume someone knows the Lord, so you do not need to witness to that person. Do not listen to Satan! Go and tell everyone the good news!

Do not always ask the Lord to do for you. Ask the Lord what you can do for Him to further His kingdom.

We must be passionate about our life in Christ.

If you are passionate about something, then it is worth doing with all of your heart and strength. Let Jesus be your passion and tell everyone why you love Him so much.

For when you have done your best in serving the Lord, still you have to keep on striving to do better far beyond that for the best of the best is still too little for such an awesome God.

The Lord says, "Whom shall I send?" If you will listen with the ear of faith say, "Here I am, Lord. Send me.

Be passionate. Never stop falling on love with Jesus!

29

The Lord Is Not Using Me Anymore

I do not belong to myself—I belong to the Lord.

We must be holy, be set apart for the Lord. This is what it takes to become a servant for the Lord.

"As free, yet not using liberty as a cloak for vice, but as bondservants of God" (1 Pet. 2:16).

Yes! We are to serve our Lord with all of our hearts; we are to be His bondservants. What an awesome, undeserving honor!

"For do I now persuade men, or God? Or do I seek to please men? For if I still pleased men, I would not be a bondservant of Christ" (Gal. 1:10).

This verse is so important! We must stop serving men! And be a bondservant for the Lord Jesus Christ. Our priorities have to be set straight. Stop focusing on pleasing man and focus only upon serving the Lord, and He will start to use you to further His kingdom.

To be more like Christ is to be a man/woman after God's own heart. We are to be a reflection of Christ—this is something we must constantly strive to do since we are His ambassadors!

Read the Word daily and pray as often as you can throughout the day. This is a great way to come into a close relationship with the Lord.

If you are waiting for the Lord to use you, you can be waiting a long time. Be in the Word everyday, and do not stop praying for the Lord to open a door to use you as His tool to further His kingdom.

The moment we stop reading His Word is when we start losing sight of Him. He does not move from us, we move from Him.

The first thing we must do in the morning is pray and then read a chapter in the Word of God. Then you can start your day. Do this every single morning and never stop!

Every night, spend at least a half hour in prayer and an hour in Bible study. You will be back on track!

30

Temptations

"Then the Lord knows how to deliver the godly out of temptations and to reserve the unjust under punishment for the day of judgment" (2 Pet. 2:9).

The Lord will never place you into temptation.

"Let no one say when he is tempted. I am tempted by God; for God cannot be tempted by evil, nor does He Himself tempt anyone. But each one is tempted when he is drawn away by his own desires and enticed" (James 1:13–14).

We must turn our back on temptation! Turn your back on the evil one, and he will flee from you.

"No temptation has overtaken you except such as is common to man; but God is faithful, who will not allow you to be tempted beyond what you are able, but with the temptation will also make the way of escape, that you may be able to bear it" (1 Cor. 10:13).

When you are tempted, the Lord will not give you more than you can handle. We must stay strong and focus upon the Lord. He will help you to overcome and the Lord will have the glory!

"Blessed is the man who endured temptation; for when he has been approved, he will receive the crown of life which the Lord has promised to those who love Him" (James 1:12).

Knowing and obeying God's Word is an effective weapon against temptation.

Also staying in constant communication with the Lord throughout the day will keep you on the right track and give you the strength to turn your back on temptation.

31

Trials

When you are going through a hard time, remember what the Lord tells us.

"Be still, and know that I am God; I will be exalted among the nations, I will be exalted in the earth!" (Ps. 46:10).

Yes, he is in control; let him handle it not you. Jesus says, "He who does not take up his cross and follow Me is not worthy of Me."

Like Job, we must overcome what Satan throws at us and never stop giving the Lord glory!

"Be of good courage, and He shall strengthen your heart, all you who hope in the LORD" (Ps. 31:24).

God will either calm the storm, or He will let the storm rage while He calms you.

The Lord will use your trials for His glory, be at peace. Jesus is in control.

Be strong! Through our hardships, the Lord will build us in character and draw us close to Him; lean upon the Lord always.

"Have I not commanded you? Be strong and of good courage; do not be afraid nor be dismayed, for the LORD your God is with you wherever you go" (Joshua 1:9).

Yes! Stand strong upon the solid rock of the Lord.

A time of trial serves to bring you to a closer relationship with the Lord, and then he will use the trials for his glory.

"I sought the LORD and He heard me and delivered me from all my fears" (Ps. 34:4).

"This poor man cried out and the LORD heard him and saved him out of all his troubles" (Ps. 34:6).

Times of trials serve to sift the true Christians from unbelievers or fair-weather Christians.

"Fear not, for I am with you; be not dismayed, for I am your God I will strengthen you, Yes, I will help you, I will uphold you with My righteous right hand" (Isa. 41:10).

We have to have trust and faith in our Lord. He is always with you. If we show fear, that shows a lack of faith. Be strong in the Lord always.

The Lord was David's shepherd; He is your shepherd and mine too. Let Him lead and guide you through your journey, give Him control…let go!

Stop running to your friends with your trials. Run to the only one who is able to help you—Jesus only Jesus. Run to Him!

"Our soul waits for the LORD; He is our help and our shield. For our heart shall rejoice in Him because we have trusted in His holy name" (Ps. 33:20–21).

We go through hard times. We must remember the Lord will not give us more than we can handle. Then He will use those times to glorify Him.

"My help comes from the LORD, who made heaven and earth" (Ps. 121:2).

Do not rely on man to help you, King David knew very well where his help comes from and we are to learn from Him. Look unto the Lord for help and only the Lord.

32

Going through Hard Times

When going through a hard time in your life, remember the words of the Lord.

"Be still and know that I am God" (Ps. 46:10a).

This verse is telling us to stop and take a step back. Look at your situation and to "be still" and to know that God is in control, not you. Let Him take control and let go of it.

We must be strong. Through our hardships, the Lord will build us in character and draw us closer to Him. We must lean upon the Lord always.

"For He shall give His angels charge over you, to keep you in all your ways" (Ps. 91:11).

The Lord gives the Lord takes away, blessed is the Lord.

We go through hard times. We must remember the Lord will not give us more than we can handle. Then He will use those times to glorify Him.

"My help comes from the LORD, who made heaven and earth" (Ps. 121:2).

Yes, our help comes from the Lord, the God who created all things.

We are to keep our eyes on heaven, upon Jesus, and He will carry us through every situation, through our life here on earth.

> The LORD is my shepherd; I shall not want. He makes me to lie down in green pastures; he leads me beside the still waters. He restores my soul; he leads me in the path of righteousness for his namesake. (Ps. 23:1–3)

Yes, the Lord is our shepherd; allow Him to lead and to guide you. You will be blessed.

If you are having a hard time in your life, remember the words of our Lord:

> Let your conduct be without covetousness; be content with such things as you have. For He Himself has said, I will never leave you nor forsake you." So we may boldly say: The LORD is my helper; I will not fear. What can man do to me?" (Heb. 13:5–6)

Run to Jesus, cling to Him, and never let go!

When going through hard times, count it as good. The Lord will use those times to build you up in your faith and to use you greater for His honor and glory.

Our hard times cannot compare what Jesus went through. When He was hanging on the cross in His anguish, our Lord did not look to His friends. Though God was angry Jesus cried out, "My God, My God." This is the only cry that should come from us. Even if God seems so far away, keep on crying out to Him. Depend on it! He will help you.

Let us learn from David.

"Truly my soul silently waits for God; From Him comes my salvation. He only is my rock and my salvation; He is my defense; I shall not be greatly moved" (Ps. 62:1–2).

Does your soul silently wait for God? Is He only your rock and your salvation? Do you stand upon the solid rock of the Lord? Do you trust in Him with all of your heart? Where does your help come from? I pray that it comes from the Lord.

"But You, O Lord, *are* a shield for me. My glory and the One who lifts up my head. I cried to the Lord with my voice and He heard me from His holy hill" (Ps. 3:3–4).

You may be going through some tough times in your life; you may even be at death's door. I am telling you to look to the crucified one, and by looking you will find that there is eternal life for you! Yes, that is a promise per the Lord Jesus Christ. There is a better life for you by trusting in Christ. Rest in Him! He promises you a peace that is beyond all understanding.

"Peace I leave with you, My peace I give to you; not as the world gives do I give to you. Let not your heart be troubled, neither let it be afraid" (John 14:27).

Jesus says, "He who does not take up his cross and follow Me is not worthy of Me."

After the storms in your life comes the sunshine. Call out to the Lord, and He will help you through the rainy season and bring you to the Son.

We must be strong through our hardships; the Lord will build us in character and draw us closer to Him. Lean upon the Lord always.

Tough times will build your character; testing times will strengthen your faith. Stay strong in the Lord.

The word *overcome* is throughout the Word of God. Jesus uses it a lot in regards to us overcoming. Like Jesus had to overcome the cross, we also have to overcome what we're going through. Then He promises us eternal life with Him. We must overcome, and the only way is to keep our eyes upon the risen Savior, the Messiah the Lord Jesus Christ, and only He will help us to overcome.

God goes on stretching you till His purpose is in sight, then He lets it fly like an arrow. Trust yourself in God's hands.

"Casting all your care upon Him, for He cares for you" (1 Pet. 5:7).

Do not put a distance between you and God during hard times; He will help you through them better than anyone else.

"Therefore humble yourselves under the mighty hand of God, that He may exalt you in due time" (1 Pet. 5:6).

33

Deception

We have to be very careful that we are not deceived.

In the body of the Lord, there are too many not following the Scripture. We cannot accept and tolerate unholy alliances. This is not glorifying the Lord.

Why do we always try to live our lives to please others and ourselves? All we do is get ourselves deeper and deeper into the hole.

Some people may know Christ's name, but they do not have His nature. Some may call Him Lord but are evildoers.

"Many will say to me that day Lord, Lord, have we not prophesied in Your name, cast out demons in Your name, and done many wonders in Your name? And then I will declare to them, I never knew you; depart from Me, you who practice lawlessness!" (Matt. 7:22–23).

Some honor all prophets. They esteem them as holding a high office and assume God must send a prophet. But for that very reason, there are many counterfeits that God has never sent. So we must watch out for false prophets.

"Woe to the rebellious children, says the Lord, who take counsel, but not of Me and who devise plans, but not of My

Spirit. That they may add sin to sin; and have not asked My advice" (Isa. 30:1–2b).

Before making any decision, we should always go to the Lord in prayer and ask Him to lead and to guide us.

Do not try to go with the majority. Truth is usually with the minority. Travel down the narrow path of the Lord, for the freeway leads to destruction.

Do not deceive yourselves by reading the Word of God and not doing what it says.

Be careful whom you bow your knee to. Who or what will we bow too? Will we serve the "gods" of this world or the God of creation? Will we serve the enticing distractions of contemporary life or the Holy One whose Name is above all names?

Remember: amateurs built the ark; professionals built the *Titanic*.

Also, we must not be deceived by our sins; we must turn our back on them or Jesus will have nothing to do with us.

James writes to us: "But be doers of the Word and not hearers only, deceiving yourselves" (James 1:22).

These are some very powerful words to live by.

Because there are so many wolves in sheep's clothing, we must deprogram ourselves and get back into the truth, God's Word.

Man will be accountable to where he leads the Lord's children astray. Someone may claim to follow Jesus, but does not know Him at all. Then you are deceived. Their personal life is filled with sin and deception.

Anything that sounds good to the ear will bring temporary satisfaction.

There are some people who invent new teachings and seem to think that Christianity is something that they may twist into any form and shape they please. They deceive many people. Yet when it happens, let us remember that our King predicted it.

> "Then they will deliver you up to tribulation and kill you and you will be hated by all nations for My name's sake. And then many will be offended, will betray one another and will hate one another. Then many false prophets will rise up and deceive many. And because lawlessness will abound, the love of many will grow cold. But he who endures to the end shall be saved. And this gospel of the kingdom will be preached in all the world as a witness to all the nations, and then the end will come." (Matt. 24:9–14)

Read your Bible everyday and know its contents so Satan will not deceive you!

Be careful who you let enter your inner circle…bad company corrupts good character. The path of least resistance is not always the way to go.

We all must be aware. We are all guilty of this. Satan, who's in charge of the world, will tempt us to be overly focused upon the sinful world because it would take our sight and our ambition off our relationship with Jesus.

Do not be hardened by the deceits of sin.

Remember, man cannot help you like the Lord can. Man can turn against you or give you false hopes. The Lord loves you enough to give His life for you.

With false teaching and loose morals comes a destructive disease, the loss of true love for God.

34

Fear

Fear of the Adversary

There are different types of fear. When we serve the Lord, we have great fear of the adversary. Our flesh wants to fear, but in Christ Jesus, there is no fear! So when fear comes, run to Jesus! Just say His name, He is always near.

We must always remember that we must conquer fear with keeping our eyes focused solely upon the Lord. If we hold on to that fear and let it fester in us, then we are not trusting in Jesus.

"Our soul waits for the LORD; He is our help and our shied" (Ps. 33:20).

"The LORD is my rock and my fortress and my deliverer; My God, my strength, in whom I will trust: My shield and the horn of my salvation, my stronghold" (Ps. 18:2–3).

Always remember the Lord is our rock; He is our fortress, and He will deliver us from what we are going through. He is our shield and our salvation. We must call upon the Lord; He is always ready to help us.

"This poor man cried out and the LORD heard him and saved him out of all his troubles. The angle of the LORD encamps all around those who fear Him and delivers them" (Ps. 34:6–7).

He will hear you when you cry out to Him.

"For God has not given us a spirit of fear, but of power and of love and of a sound mind. Therefore do not be ashamed of the testimony of our Lord" (2 Tim. 1:7–8a).

When you feel like you are all alone, you are not! Jesus tells us that He is with us always. Call out to Him, He is there and He wants to hear from you.

"But You, O LORD, are a shield for me, my glory and the One who lifts up my head. I cried to the LORD with my voice and He heard me from His holy hill" (Ps. 3:3–4).

Yes, cry out to the Lord in spirit and in truth, for the Lord is spirit. He promises that He will hear you and He will help; stand strong.

"The eyes of the LORD are on the righteous, and His ears are open to their cry" (Ps. 34:15).

Serving the Lord on the front lines of the spiritual battlefield is hard, but an awesome honor. You will be going through a hard time; Satan and his friends keep on beating you up. The Lord encourages us with this verse: "Fear not, for I am with you; be not dismayed, for I am your God. I will strengthen you, Yes, I will help you, I will uphold you with My righteous right hand" (Isa. 41:10).

What an awesome God we have!

Do not be dismayed and have courage because the God we serve is with us.

Look what God will do:

> He is with us,
> He will strengthen us,
> He will help us,
> He will uphold us with His powerful right hand.

In this verse alone, we have four things God will do for us. This is the reason we can and must move forward. We must not fear!

Continue to give glory to God in your suffering, and He will restore you. You will be strong in the Lord.

"Be strong and of good courage, do not fear nor be afraid of them; for the LORD your God, He is the One who goes with you. He will not leave you nor forsake you" (Deut. 31:6).

Our flesh wants to fear. But in Christ Jesus, there is no fear! So when fear comes, run to Jesus! Just say His name; He is always near.

When I am afraid, I will trust in the Lord.

"Be of good courage and He shall strengthen your heart, all you who hope in the LORD" (Ps. 31:24).

If God is for us, then who can be against us?

Always keep in mind: my help comes from the Lord, the maker of heaven and earth. It does not get any better than this.

"In the day when I cried out, You answered me and made me bold with strength in my soul" (Ps. 138:3).

In our distress, we will call out to the Lord and He will hear.

"Therefore submit to God. Resist the devil and he will flee from you" (James 4:7).

We must turn our back on Satan and he will flee! We have protection!

"Do not rejoice over me, my enemy; when I fall, I will arise; when I sit in darkness, the LORD will be a light to me" (Mic. 7:8).

Keep this verse of encouragement with you always. When we are pushed over the edge and fall, we will arise! When we sit in darkness, the Lord is our light! Be encouraged, my friends! The Lord is with you!

If Satan is not attacking you, then you are not a threat to him. If you do not have his attention, then you are not serving the Lord.

"Beloved, do not think it strange concerning the fiery trial which is to try you, as though some strange thing happened to you; But rejoice to the extent that you partake of Christ's sufferings, that when His glory is revealed, you may also be glad with exceeding joy" (1 Pet. 4:12–13).

Remember the words of David: "Whenever I am afraid, I will trust in You" (Ps. 56:3).

Do not trust in man, keep your eyes upon the Lord and trust in Him only.

"What then shall we say to these things? If God is for us, who can be against us?" (Rom. 8:31).

"My help comes from the LORD, Who made heaven and earth" (Ps. 121:2).

Do not ever look for your help to come from anyone else, only from the Lord.

"The righteous cry out and the LORD hears and delivers them out of all their troubles" (Ps. 34:17).

"On the day when I cried out; You answered me and made me bold with strength in my soul" (Ps. 138:3).

Jesus promises us a peace that is beyond all understanding: "Peace I leave with you, My peace I give to you; not as the world gives do I give to you. Let not your heart be troubled, neither let it be afraid" (John 14:27).

Do not be afraid to go out of your comfort zone. If the Lord opens the door, go! He will be with you.

"I called on the LORD in distress; The LORD answered me and set me in a broad place. The LORD is on my side; I will not fear. What can man do to me?" (Ps. 118:5–6).

"It is better to trust in the LORD than to put confidence in man" (Ps. 118:8).

"In my distress I cried to the LORD, and He heard me" (Ps. 120:1).

Yes, just like the Lord would hear David in his distress, He will also hear you. Do not fear, have faith.

Always remember, do not let the evil one get the best of you! We do not want to let the Lord down.

"Now the just shall live by faith: but if anyone draws back, My soul has no pleasure in him" (Heb. 10:38).

I hope this verse will encourage you to stand strong upon the Lord and glorify Him!

God is protecting you for deliverance! We have protection! Do not fear; fearing shows unbelief in the Lord. A holy fear mixed with fullness of joy is one of the sweetest compounds we can bring to the Lord.

"God is our refuge and strength, a very present help on trouble, therefore we will not fear" (Ps. 46:1–2a).

Stay strong in the Lord; He is with us always.

"In God (I will praise His Word), In God I have put my trust; I will not fear. What can flesh do to me?" (Ps. 56:4).

So, the Lord is using you; that is so awesome! If you have the attention of Satan, then you are doing a wonderful job! Praise the Lord! Remember if we serve the Lord, we are fighting a spiritual battle. Do not run to man, only run to the Lord.

"Truly my soul silently waits for God; from Him comes my salvation. He only is my rock and my salvation; He is my defense; I shall not be greatly moved" (Ps. 62:1–2).

Like David, our soul is to silently wait for God, and from Him comes our salvation. He is our rock and our salvation and our defense; we shall not be moved. Stand strong upon the Lord. Do not be afraid of what is ahead; just follow the leading of the Lord, run through that open door and serve Him where He leads you.

"Every word of God is pure; He is a shield to those who put their trust in Him" (Ps. 30:5).

The Lord will help us against the enemy; human help is worthless. With God on our side, we will win.

"Give us help from trouble, for the help of man is useless. Through God we will do valiantly. For it is He who shall tread down our enemies" (Ps. 60:11–12).

Wait upon the Lord!

"The Lord is my light and my salvation; Whom shall I fear? The Lord is the strength of my life; of whom shall I be afraid?" (Psalm 27:1).

"Have I not commanded you? Be strong and of good courage; do not be afraid, nor be dismayed, for the Lord your God is with you wherever you go" (Joshua 1:9).

The Lord is not just talking to Joshua; He is talking to you also.

"In the day when I cried out You answered me and made me bold with strength in my soul" (Ps. 138:3).

We must cry out to the Lord; we must not rely on man for man is weak. Run only to the Lord. We have to just stop! We must compose ourselves and focus on God.

"Be still and know that I am God" (Ps. 47:10).

My first book, *Encouragement,* will be a big help in your time of being attacked by Satan. I highly recommend it.

Fear of God

There are so many people that take advantage of the Lord. They just live their lives and do not care anything about going against His wishes. Yes, we have a loving and a caring God, but he warns us time after time about going against His Word. We are to fear the Almighty God!

"Therefore you shall keep the commandments of the LORD your God, to walk in His ways and to fear Him" (Deut. 8:6).

Abraham feared the LORD and was frightful when he would come into a town and did not think that they feared the LORD.

"And Abram said, because I thought, surely the fear of God is not in this place; and they will kill me on account of my wife" (Gen. 20:11).

Joseph (the son of Jacob) feared the Lord and did his best to please Him.

"Then Joseph said to them the third day. Do this and live, for I fear God" (Gen. 42:18).

Moses was overwhelmed with counseling all of the people of Israel. Then Jethro, Moses's father-in-law, gave him some sound advice.

"Moreover you shall select from all the people able men, such as fear God, men of truth, hating covetousness; and place such over them to be rulers of thousands, rulers of hundreds, rulers of fifties and rulers of tens" (Exo. 18:21).

Note the people Moses was to choose to help him had to fear God. The Lord Himself is telling us to fear Him.

"You shall not curse the deaf, nor put a stumbling block before the blind, but shall fear your God: I am the Lord" (Lev. 19:14).

The Lord tells us to honor the presence of an old man and to fear the Lord.

"You shall rise before the gray headed and honor the presence of an old man and fear your God: I am the Lord" (Lev. 19:32).

In the book of Deuteronomy, the Lord tells us to learn to fear Him and to teach our children to fear God.

"That they may learn to fear Me all the days they live on the earth, and that they may teach their children" (Deut. 4:10b).

"And the Lord commanded us to observe all these statutes, to fear the Lord our God, for our good always" (Deut. 6:24a).

We are to fear the Lord and stand in awe of Him. Do we do this today? Have we taught our children to fear the Lord and to stand in awe of the Almighty God? We need to get back to Scripture, to learn how to live our lives according to the Word of God.

"Let all the earth fear the Lord; let all the inhabitants of the world stand in awe of Him" (Ps. 33:8).

The Almighty God created all things; we are to stand in awe Him. We are to give Him praise and glory we are to shower Him with blessings for He is so worthy.

"This poor man cried out and the Lord heard him and saved him out of all his troubles. The angel of the Lord encamps all around those who fear Him and delivers them" (Ps. 34:6–7).

"For You, O God, have heard my vows; You have given me the heritage of those who fear Your name" (Ps. 61:5).

Yes, that is for you and for me. If we fear the Lord God Almighty, we have an everlasting heritage, per the Lord Himself.

"So he said to them, "I am a Hebrew; and I fear the Lord, the God of heaven, who made the sea and the dry land" (Jonah 1:9).

"And do not fear those who kill the body but cannot kill the soul. But rather fear Him who is able to destroy both soul and body in hell" (Matt. 10:28).

"Then the churches throughout all Judea, Galilee, and Samaria had peace and were edified, and walking in the fear of the Lord and in the comfort of the Hoy Spirit, they were multiplied" (Acts 9:31).

"Therefore, having these promises, beloved, let us cleanse ourselves from all filthiness of the flesh and spirit, perfecting holiness in the fear of God" (2 Cor. 7:1).

We are to fear the Almighty God.

"The fear of the Lord is the beginning of wisdom" (Ps. 111:10).

"For as the heavens are high above the earth, so great is His mercy toward those who fear Him" (Ps. 103:11).

We must have a genuine fear of God.

"By faith Noah, being divinely warned of things not yet seen, moved with godly fear, prepared an ark for the saving of his household. By which he condemned the world and became heir of the righteousness which is according to faith" (Heb. 11:7).

Even though Noah never saw the Lord, he followed the Lord's instructions by fear and faith. We need the fear and the faith in the Lord that Noah had.

In the book of Revelation, John writes that he saw an angel flying in heaven, "saying with a loud voice, 'Fear God and give glory to Him, for the hour of His judgment has come; and worship Him who made heaven and earth, the sea and springs of water'" (Rev. 14:7).

We are all to fear the Almighty God and give Him the glory that He deserves. His judgment of us will be everlasting.

"He will fulfill the desire of those who fear Him; He also will hear their cry and save them. The LORD preserves all who love Him" (Ps. 145:19–20a).

35

There Is a War Going On!

We as followers of Jesus Christ are in the middle of a spiritual battle. When we serve our Lord, Satan and his demons are actively at war against you; it is called spiritual warfare. The only way we can make it is to have our eyes constantly upon Jesus, and he will help us through it and be glorified through it.

When we serve our Lord, Satan will take notice and attack us. Keep your eyes upon the Lord and turn your back on Satan and he will flee.

> Finally, my brethren, be strong in the Lord and in the power of His might. Put on the whole armor of God that you may be able to stand against the wiles of the devil. For we do not wrestle against flesh and blood, but against principalities, against powers against the rulers of the darkness of this age, against spiritual hosts of wickedness in the heavenly places. Therefore take up the whole armor of God, that you may be able to withstand in the evil day and having done all to stand. (Eph. 6:10–13)

We must overcome what Satan throws at us and never stop giving the Lord praise and glory! Show Satan whose side you're on.

Always remember, the Lord will not give us more than we can handle. Serve Him with all of your heart. He knows where to place you in your service for Him.

The more we are a witness for the Lord, the more we get the attention of Satan. He will hit you hard. Keep your eyes upon Jesus; He will help you.

Pray for knowledge and wisdom to serve the Lord better and stronger, He will supply all we need; we just have to ask.

"He who is in you is greater than he who is in the world" (1 John 4:4b).

We must witness with boldness, stand firm upon the solid rock of our Savior Jesus the Christ. He is our refuge and salvation.

Turn your back on Satan, and he will flee. We belong to Jesus; through Him we have authority over the evil one! Stand strong in the Lord!

Do not glorify Satan. When he tries to get you to back down from witnessing for our Lord, show him who you serve and keep him under your feet.

Declare with me today: I have strength and grace for breakthrough and victory! Every enemy and challenge is defeated! In Jesus's name, it is so! Amen.

Do not give Satan any glory today by withholding your love for the Lord. Witness to as many people as you can! God Bless You All!

Our hope is in Christ Jesus.

Tell Satan to "get out of the way!"

We serve the Almighty God, the God who created all creation, the Almighty God! Blessed is the Lord.

Do not forget: when we go through spiritual warfare, never stop praising the Lord!

Serve the Lord with all of your heart today. Show the world that you live for the Lord! Place Satan under your feet, and you will not be moved!

When someone would come up against you today, shower them with love. Be a reflection of Jesus to them, love them like Jesus would.

Tell as many people as you can what Jesus means to you, tell them why you love Jesus so much. Give Him glory and honor today.

You serve the Lord. You do not understand why you are where you are. You are way outside of your comfort zone. It is okay; Jesus placed you there; just go!

"Trust in the Lord with all your heart and lean not on your own understanding; in all your ways acknowledge Him and He shall direct your paths" (Proverbs 3:5–6).

Just trust in Him. We will never understand the ways of the Lord; we are to just trust and follow His lead. Let Him use you where He has placed you.

"Fear not, for I am with you Be not dismayed, for I am your God. I will strengthen you, Yes, I will help you, I will uphold you with My righteous right hand" (Isa. 41:10).

Spiritual warfare is real! I have been in the thick of it.

My first book, *Encouragement*, will help you. I have an excellent chapter on spiritual warfare that is a must for anyone going through the battle!

36

Satan Is Real

"Be sober, be vigilant; because your adversary the devil walks about like a roaring lion, seeking whom he may devour" (1 Pet. 5:8).

Be self-controlled and alert. Resist him and stand firm in your faith in Jesus Christ.

Satan will try as hard as he can to stop you from being a witness for the Lord. Do not give him the glory! Turn your back on him and he will flee.

We belong to Jesus; through Him we have authority over the evil one! Stand strong in the Lord!

The moment we take our eyes off of Jesus, that is a calling card for Satan to come into your life—do not let that happen.

Let your light shine for the Lord today. Do not hold back, holding back will only glorify Satan.

Do not glorify Satan when he tries to get you to back down from witnessing for our Lord. Show him who you serve and keep Satan under your feet.

It is good to keep tabs on ourselves. To see how we are walking, to make sure we did not fall into Satan's trap of worldliness.

Do not let Satan pull the wool over your eyes! With all the attention with "gay rights" Satan is in his glory!

> "Therefore God also gave them up to uncleanness, in the lusts of their hearts, to dishonor their bodies among themselves, who exchanged the truth of God for the lie and worshiped and served the creature rather than the Creator, who is blessed forever. Amen. For this reason God gave them up to vile passions. For even their women exchanged the natural use for what is against nature. Likewise also the men, leaving the natural use of the woman, burned in their lust for one another, men with men committing what is shameful and receiving in themselves the penalty of their error which was due." (Rom. 1:24–27)

"Who, knowing the righteous judgment of God, that those who practice such things are deserving of death, not only do the same but also approve of those who practice them" (Rom. 1:32).

Do not ever forget these verses. Paul tells us that even if we approve of those sinful actions, we will be deserving of death. Be careful! We must not approve of such actions. Death is eternal separation from God!

Do you go against the Ten Commandments and say the Lord understands? No. He does not. Do not let Satan pull the wool over your eyes.

You really do not want to spend eternity with Satan and his gang! Turn your back on the world and serve the Lord.

Are you giving Satan all the glory in your life with your lifestyle? Live for Jesus.

Satan and the demons are your foes and are not in any way your friends! Our only hope is in Christ Jesus.

Satan wants to bring death to everything in your life, including your love, joy, marriage, and especially your soul.

Be careful. When Satan sees you serving the Lord, he will try to stop you by tempting you in the world. Just turn your back on him and he will flee.

> "How you are fallen from heaven, O Lucifer, son of the morning! How you are cut down to the ground, you who weakened the nations! For you have said in your heart; I will ascend into heaven, I will exalt my throne above the stars of God; I will also sit on the mount of the congregation on the farthest sides of the north; I will ascend above the heights of the clouds, I will be like the Most High. Yet you shall be brought down to Sheol, to the lowest depths of the Pit." (Isa. 14:12–15)

37

Stand Firm

Be strong. Through our hardships, the Lord will build us in character and draw us closer to Him. We must lean upon the Lord always.

We must never stop witnessing with boldness. Stand firm upon the solid rock of our Savior Jesus the Christ. He is our refuge and salvation.

Sometimes we feel like we are being beat up by the world. It is okay! Jesus had it worse. When we are being attacked by the evil one—that means we have his attention. That is great! This means we are doing a good job for the Lord, and He is glorified!

When Satan leaves us alone, this means we are not a threat to him, we are not doing our job for our Lord.

With Jesus at our side, Satan does not stand a chance.

Let us not be ashamed. Stand up for what you believe. Jesus, yes, Jesus.

Jesus is the Messiah, Lord above all lords. He's our redeemer, our refuge, our solid rock. Stand firm upon the solid rock of the Messiah.

He did not promise us a rose garden, but He did promise us that He would never leave us.

Stand strong upon the Word of the Lord.

A man does not win souls to Christ while he is himself half asleep. Men who are made alive through the Spirit of God must fight the battle that is to be fought for the Lord Jesus.

"This is a faithful saying: For if we died with Him, we shall also live with Him. If we endure, we shall also reign with Him. If we deny Him, He also will deny us" (2 Tim. 2:11–12).

We all have a race to run for our Lord. Let us run it as fast as we can with victory in our sights. To give Jesus full honor and glory

We must have a close relationship with Jesus; we will be powerless without Him.

You look around and all you see is sin and evil all around you. What do you do? Ask the Lord to use you as his warrior where he has placed you.

God has to take us into the valley and put us through fire to reshape us so we will be able to be used greatly by Him. Stand firm upon the Lord.

Pray for protection from the enemy; we need it when we are on the front lines of the battlefield, fighting for our Lord.

Do not give up! Jesus did not. Do not let Satan sneak in the back door; he will try. Keep your eyes fixed always upon Jesus.

If we serve the Lord, we will get the attention of Satan. Stay in prayer and turn your back on Satan; he will flee. Be strong in the Lord. Do not hold back your witness for Him. Tell as many people as possible why you love Jesus so much! Glorify Him!

38

Trust in the Lord

Trust in the Lord and only the Lord. Do not try to understand where the Lord is leading you, just go and honor Him. It is between you and Him only. Do not go running to anyone else! Run only to the Lord.

"To You O Lord, I lift up my soul; in You I trust, O my God" (Ps. 25:1).

Like King David, we are to lift everything we have up to the Lord. We are to trust in Him and not in man. To the God who created you and me, who created all. Think about it. God put you together while you were still in your mother's womb. You are made in His image. He created the air that you breathe, the sun, moon, skies, clouds, the different seasons we have, and the trees, flowers, and the water we drink. We have such an awesome God! He deserves us to lift all we have up to Him and to put our entire trust in Him. No one could ever love us more then the Lord. The reason He created you was to have a personal relationship with Him. Such an unworthy honor that people do not pursue.

We need to live for God, to trust Him. Do not say what if this and what if that, then you are not trusting God. You need to be radical for Him.

If any of you lacks wisdom, let him ask of God, who gives to all liberally and without reproach and it will be given to him. All we have to do is ask.

In his heart, a man plans his course, but the Lord determines his steps.

The Lord tells us in Scripture "not to put your trust in man."

> This is what the LORD says: Cursed is the one who trusts in man, who depends on flesh for his strength and whose heart turns away from the LORD. He will be like a bush in the wastelands; he will not see prosperity when it comes, He will dwell in the parched places of the desert in a salt land where no one lives.
>
> But blessed is the man who trusts in the LORD, whose confidence is in Him. He will be like a tree planted by water that sends out its roots by the stream. It does not fear when heat comes; its leaves are always green it has no worried in a year of drought and never fails to bear fruit. (Jeremiah 17:5–8, NIV)

We must trust in the Lord and not man. Our confidence is to be in Him only. We then will be like a tree planted by the stream and be protected by the Lord. We are to bear fruit for the Lord. That means to witness, to be a reflection of Christ everyday.

These are very wise words from Oswald Chambers:

> If God has made your cup sweet, drink it with grace, if He has made it bitter; drink it in communion with Him.

If the order of God for you is a hard time, go
through it,
   But never choose the scene of your martyrdom.

Be careful not to plan your own course of serving the Lord.
He has His own plan for you. Just ask Him to lead you.

"Truly my soul silently waits for God; From Him comes
my salvation. He only is my rock and my salvation; He is
my defense; I shall not be greatly moved" (Ps. 62:1–2).

Does your soul silently wait for God? Is He only your
rock and your salvation? Do you stand upon the solid rock
of the Lord? Do you trust in Him with all of our heart?
Where does your help come from? I pray that is comes
from the Lord.

Put your trust in the Lord. He is our portion now and
forever. In good times and in bad, the Lord in control, run
to Him!

The Lord gives; the Lord takes away. Bless is the Lord! He
is in control.

Humble yourself before your God, turn your back on
worldliness, and live for Him, not the sinful world. We are
not to put our trust in anyone but God.

We are to make Jesus our ruler and King, trusting Him
totally and allowing Him to make us whole. He will totally
change our life.

We serve a God of restoration. God restored Joseph, placed
him as ruler of Egypt. Then God restored Joseph to his
family, yes! We have a God of restoration, we must trust
in Him.

It is much easier to do something than to trust in God; we must not mistake panic for inspiration.

So many times we just do not understand, but it is okay! If we serve the Lord, He tells us to trust in Him and not in our own understanding.

"Trust in the LORD with all your heart and lean not on your own understanding; in all your ways acknowledge Him and He shall direct your paths" (Proverbs 3:5–6).

A question I am often asked is: why does God permit His people to endure persecution?

- It acts as a sieve to sift the church of its hypocrites.
- It reveals the reality of our conversion experiences.
- It will take our eyes off of the world and focus upon Jesus once again.
- It will bring us into a close relationship with the Lord.
- It also does us good, as painful as our persecutions are; they drive us to prayer.

Place your trust in God and believe that there is nothing too hard for God.

39

Love

Jesus loves you more than anyone else could ever love you. Seek Him and you will find Him. Then cling to Him with every bit of strength you have and never let go! He wants you to be His ambassador, just say yes to the Lord and run down the path He has laid out for your life.

Unworthy as we are, he loves us still in Christ and looks upon us not as we are in ourselves, but as we are in Him—washed in His blood and covered in His righteousness.

You must love the Lord your God more than anyone else, more than your own life.

"But it is written: Eye has not seen, nor ear heard, nor have entered into the heart of man the things which God has prepared for those who love Him" (1 Cor. 2:9).

The Lord loves us more than anyone could ever love us. "But God demonstrates His own love toward us, in that while we were still sinners, Christ died for us" (Rom. 5:8).

Yes, He gave His life for you and for me. Do we owe Him a sinful life (slapping Him in the face)? Or does He deserve our life, for Him to use us for His glory?

With false teaching and loose morals comes a destructive disease the loss of true love for God.

Love is so amazing. No love can ever compare to the Love Jesus has for you. Never take your eyes off of the Lord.

"Pray without ceasing" (2 Thess. 5:17).

The King is coming! Jesus is so loving He gave His life for us. Not only that, He calls us His friends; and if that were not enough, He invites us to be His bride and live with Him forever. That is the depth of His love.

"Set your mind on things above, not on things on the earth" (Col. 3:2).

He desires our love, in return for His love for us.

God loves us no matter what we have done; He gives us a second chance. Holy is the Lord.

The definition of love is what Jesus did for us—He died for us. We must die to ourselves and live for Him.

No one can ever love you more than the Lord. He is the only one who freely gave his life for you, and by His blood your sins are totally washed away!

Love the Lord with all of your heart. Everything and everyone else is second. Do not ever put anyone or anything above your love for the Lord.

> "I will love You, O Lord, my strength. The Lord is my rock and my fortress and my deliverer; My God, my strength, in whom I will trust; My shield and the horn of my salvation, my stronghold. I will

call upon the LORD, who is worthy to be praised."
(Ps. 18:1–3a)

Yes, love Him with all of your heart. Let Him know how thankful you are for everything He does for you. We are to serve the one we love with all our hearts. Jesus, Jesus, Jesus. Never stop telling people why you love Him so much.

We have to prove our love for the Lord through being used by Him as His tool. Do not let a day go by without witnessing to someone.

No one can ever love you more than Jesus. He deserves our all.

Let us go back to our first love for God! He loves us passionately, but sometimes we lose our flame for Him.

Father, never have we experienced love like Yours. We are a thankful people. You give us Your faithful love here and will see us safely home.

40

Truth

God is truth.

"Lead me in Your truth and teach me, for you are the God of my salvation; on You I wait all the day" (Ps. 25:5).

Like King David, this should be our constant prayer.

"All the paths of the LORD are mercy and truth. To such as keep His covenant and His testimonies" (Ps. 25:10).

Read your Bible daily to gain an understanding of the great Creator and what He requires of you.

"Only fear the LORD and serve Him in truth with all your heart; for consider what great things He has done for you" (1 Sam. 12:24).

"Lead me in Your truth and teach me. For You are the God of my salvation: On You I wait all the day" (Ps. 24:10).

As King David would pour his heart out to the Lord, we should learn from him. We should cry out to the Lord, "Lead me in Your truth, O Lord, and teach me!"

"For Your mercy reaches unto the heavens, and Your truth unto the clouds" (Ps. 57:11).

We are to love truth. All that have taken their pleasure in wickedness will be condemned.

"And the LORD passed before him and proclaimed, The LORD the LORD God, merciful and gracious, longsuffering, and abounding in goodness and truth'" (Exod. 34:6).

The eternal God the God of all creation is abounding in goodness and truth.

There is so much in this world that contaminates us. We need to be filled with purity and truth.

You can start a lie, but you cannot stop it. There is no telling how long it will live. Let us never teach even the least bit of error to a little child. For it may live on and will be accepted long after we are dead. There is not any limit to its life and power. Nothing lives as long as a lie—except the truth.

Do not try to go with the majority. Truth is usually with the minority. Travel down the narrow path of the Lord, the freeway leads to destruction.

We must live our lives in purity and in truth.

"God is Spirit, and those who worship Him must worship in spirit and truth" (John 4:24).

"And you shall know the truth, and the truth shall make you free" (John 8:32).

The Holy Spirit leads us into all truth. People do not put their trust in Him. To have an appetite for truth is to know the Lord more. Increase your personal quiet time with the Lord.

"And they will turn their ears away from the truth, and be turned aside to fables" (2 Tim. 4:4).

We need to remove unholy alliances in our lives if we are to have an appetite for truth.

"If we say that we have no sin, we deceive ourselves and the truth is not in us" (1 John 1:8).

"He who says, I know Him and does not keep His commandments is a liar and the truth is not in him" (1 John 2:4).

We are living in a world without truth. The Bible is truth.

"I have no greater joy than to hear that my children walk in truth" (3 John 1:4).

To please the Lord, we must all walk in truth.

Our salvation depends on biblical truth. The Lord is looking into our hearts for truth. We must get real and seek truth unto the Lord. Develop and maintain biblical truth. Encourage and strengthen our relationship with Him. Do not have any unholy alliances.

41

Prayer

Did you pray this morning? Stop what you are doing and pray with all of your heart.

Never start your day without communication with Jesus. Do not leave Him out. You will be blessed.

To gain a close relationship with the Lord, we need prayer, not just for two seconds at night, but throughout the day.

"The eyes of the LORD are on the righteous and His ears are open to their cry" (Ps. 34:15).

When we cry out to the Lord in prayer, we have a guarantee that the Lord hears us!

"The righteous cry out and the LORD hears, and delivers them out of all their troubles" (Ps. 34:17).

We need to pray if all hope is lost. When people are against us, when we are fearful and weak, we need to pray. Go to Jesus in constant prayer.

"Rejoice always, pray without ceasing" (1 Thess. 5:16–17).

Yes, we are to rejoice always in every situation, to keep on praising the Lord. With the help of the Holy Spirit, we can pray without ceasing. Yes, it is possible, and it will bring you to a close relationship with the Lord. We have an awesome God!

We are able to go into the Lord's throne room in every time of need. Do not overlook this awesome privilege.

God is always listening; talk to Him throughout the day.

"Hear my prayer, O LORD give ear to my supplications! In Your faithfulness answer me. And in Your righteousness" (Ps. 143:1).

Never believe your case is hopeless so long as you plead with God for help. If you do not see God answering your prayer, look beyond, there might be a greater blessing coming your way!

We must always pray and not forget. Pray in the time of difficulty, pray through impossible times, pray against death and the devil, and pray like Jonah when he was in the belly of the fish. Pray without ceasing. He wants to hear from us; He is the God who hears our prayers. Do not misread the Word of God. It does not forbid you to pray; the Lord has said, "I have heard your prayer. I have seen your tears."

Always remember: the victory is won through prayer!

If prayer is your companion, you will not have to say, "It is me again, Lord." When you start to pray, you will have a direct line that goes straight to heaven, where our Lord is always waiting to hear your prayer.

If we are filled with love toward God, then our desire to honor Him will be a continual prayer on our lips.

"For where two or three are gathered together in My name, I am there in the midst of them" (Matt. 18:20).

Read Psalm 4. In this Psalm of David, we can learn how to pray.

1. Ask God for an answer. David says, "Hear me when I call, O God of my righteousness!"

2. We must not forget we are sinners saved by grace and we need His mercy so we pray. "Be merciful to me and hear my prayer."

3. We must come with full confidence. "The Lord will hear when I call to Him. Trust in the Lord."

4. Now comes the breakthrough. "Let the light of your face shine upon us, O Lord. You have filled my heart with greater joy. I will lie down and sleep in peace, for you alone, O Lord, will make me dwell in safety."

Faith is now complete and the answer is on the way.

Are we neglecting our prayer time?

Praying and being in constant contact with the Lord. Brings about refreshing times and gives us strength.

You cannot witness; you just cannot do it. I was like that a long time ago. Pray and ask the Holy Spirit to give you the boldness to witness. He will!

When praying, do not just use routine words. We are to pray with all of our hearts. The Lord tells us through Paul: "I desire therefore that the men pray everywhere, lifting up holy hands, without wrath and doubting" (1 Tim. 2:8).

"Give ear to my words, O Lᴏʀᴅ, consider my meditation. Give heed to the voice of my cry. My King and my God, for to You I will pray" (Ps. 5:1–2).

Lord, lead us and guide us down the road that You want us to go down; to be used by You as Your tool to further Your kingdom. Thank you Lord! Woe to the rebellious children, says the Lord, who take counsel, but not of Me.

Do not run to your friends for counsel. Go to the Lord in prayer and ask Him to lead and to guide you.

"If I regard iniquity in my heart, the Lord will not hear. But certainly God has heard me; He has attended to the voice of my prayer. Blessed be God, who has not turned away my prayer, nor His mercy from me!" (Ps. 66:18–20).

Remember, if there is iniquity in your heart, the Lord will not hear your prayer. You must come to the throne room with a pure and clean heart.

Always remember to be righteous.

42

God the Father

"He preserves the souls of His saints; He delivers them out of the hand of the wicked. Light is sown for the righteous, and gladness for the upright in heart. Rejoice in the Lord, you righteous, and give thanks at the remembrance of His holy name" (Ps. 97:10–12).

"The Lord is my shepherd; I shall not want" (Ps. 23:1).

The Lord is your shepherd and my shepherd. We are to let Him lead and guide us in our lives just like a shepherd leads and guides his flock.

The government turns their back on God and His laws and when everything goes haywire and disaster happens, they cry, "where is God?"

Our lives are not to be controlled by our evil impulses. We need a relationship with the Lord everyday. The only way is to submit our lives to the Lord.

The Lord is the Living God. He does not change, we do.

Our failure to live according to God's expectation has caused a separation between God and us. We can get that relationship back by reading the Word of God (the Bible) and living what you read. Pray for understanding. You will gain that close relationship with Jesus. Your life will never be the same!

Not knowing God is like not knowing your mother or father—it leaves a hole in your soul that can only be filled by discovering where you have come from. The only way to know God is by reading the Bible.

The Almighty God calls us to join an army that will bring the Gospel into enemy territory.

God is always listening, talk to Him throughout the day.

"In God we boast all day long and praise Your name forever" (Ps. 44:8).

We are to learn from the writings of the Psalms. We also should boast in God all day long and never stop praising Him.

God gives and God takes away; do not take anything for granted.

Do not allow anything to rival your good judgment or your affections, but cry out to the Lord.

"O God, You are my God; early will I seek You" (Ps. 63:1a).

"So the LORD said to Moses, I will also do this thing that you have spoken; for you have found grace in My sight and I know you by name" (Exod. 33:17).

King David knew very well that the Lord knew him (us) even before we were even born.

"For you formed my inward parts: You covered me in my mother's womb. I will praise You, for I am fearfully and wonderfully made."(Ps. 139:13–14a).

Always remember the Lord knows you by name. He put you together before you were ever born. We are to strive for a personal relationship with the Lord of all creation. Our heart is to know the Lord—this should be our ultimate goal in life. We must be very careful not to put God in a box, and do not limit Him.

We are to run to the Lord God of all creation and give Him the honor that He deserves.

> I will praise You O LORD, among the peoples and I will sing praises to You among the nations. For Your mercy is great above the heavens and Your truth reaches to the clouds. Be exalted, O God above the heavens and Your glory above all the earth. (Ps. 108:3–5)

Be careful whom you bow your knee to:

To whom or to what will we bow? Will we serve the "gods" of this world or the God of creation? Will we serve the enticing distractions of contemporary life or the Holy One whose Name is above all names?

With false teaching and loose morals comes a destructive disease, the loss of true love for God.

Therefore whoever does not practice righteousness is not of God.

Do you feel very far away from God? The Lord says to us in Scripture: draw near to God, and He will draw near to you.

I know that we have a God that restores.

Father, never have we experienced love like Yours. We are a thankful people. You give us Your faithful love here and will see us safely home.

God's glory was poured into the baby of Bethlehem; it was all so frail and so unexpected. But it is also the light of God's glory that brightens every dark corner of our lives.

No one else can take the Lord's place. Make a place for the Lord in your heart. You are our God, and we bow down before You. We will lift up the name of Adonai!

"Whom have I in heaven but You? And there is none upon earth that I desire besides You. My flesh and my heart fail; but God is the strength of my heart and my portion forever" (Ps. 73:25–26).

The Lord knows you by name. He knows the number of hairs upon your head. He knows when we are sleeping and when we are awake. We cannot go from His presence. If we ascend into the heavens, He is there. If we go into the deepest sea, He is there. If we sit in the darkness, the darkness is like light to the Lord. We have such an awesome God.

"You will guide me with Your counsel and afterward receive me to glory" (Ps. 73:24).

Be very careful that your God is not money, material things, or family. None of those can take away your sins or promise you eternal life.

"The Lord by wisdom founded the earth; by understanding He established the heavens; by His knowledge the depths were broken up, and clouds drop down the dew" (Proverbs 3:19–20).

I love the Word of God! Even though you cannot always speak of heavenly things to people, you can to God!

"Ask and it will be given to you; seek and you will find; knock and it will be opened to you. For everyone who asks receives and he who seeks finds and to him who knocks it will be opened" (Matt. 7:7–8).

The spoken Word of God created the universe; He created everything. There was no big bang! God spoke.

"By faith we understand that the worlds were framed by the Word of God, so that the things which are seen were not made of things which are visible" (Heb. 11:3).

We are not to take the Almighty God for granted; we are not to treat Him as common. He is the great Creator. We are to prepare everyday throughout our lives here on earth for the great day of judgment.

Know therefore that the Lord your God is God.

"For this is God, our God forever and ever; He will be our guide even to death" (Ps. 48:14).

What are you running from? You cannot run from God.

What an undeserved privilege it is for us, as small as we are, to be able to serve the Creator of all things. To be used by the Almighty God.

"Truly my soul silently *waits* for God; from Him *comes* my salvation. He only *is* my rock and my salvation; *He is* my defense; I shall not be greatly moved" (Ps. 62:1–2).

If I want to go to God, I need a ladder that reaches all the way up to God. Jesus Christ is that ladder, for He is God in the flesh.

"God is Spirit, and those who worship Him must worship in spirit and truth" (John 4:24).

Our God is the living God.

Our God is a God of great miracles.

"For He shall give His angels charge over you, to keep you in all your ways" (Ps. 91:11).

You are never alone. Praise the Lord.

Oh Lord, You are worthy to have glory, honor, and power! You created all things.

"Blessed is the man whom You instruct, O LORD" (Ps. 94:12a).

We must be open to the Lord's instruction of our service for Him.

We have a loving God, but we also have a jealous God. Always put the Lord first in everything you do. Do not love anything or anyone more than the Lord.

"Today, if you will hear His voice: Do not harden your hearts as in the rebellion" (Ps. 95:8).

God does not walk out on us; we leave Him. Open the Word of God, read, pray, and obey.

"For I am persuaded that neither death nor life, nor angels nor principalities nor powers, nor things present nor things to come. Nor height nor depth, nor any other created thing shall be able to separate us from the love of God which is in Christ Jesus our Lord" (Rom. 8:38–39).

What does the Lord require of us? To do justly, to love mercy, and to walk humbly with our God. Also we are to "be holy for He is holy."

The Lord wants to give us an undivided heart and put a new spirit in us. He will remove from us our heart of stone and give us a heart of flesh. We will then live by His rules. We have to be changed from the inside out. This is the only way we can please the Almighty God.

Our sacrifice to God is a broken spirit. Beyond the traditions of our culture, it should be a return to God. We are to put materialism in second place.

God wants to dwell with us. He wants to live in us. Everything in our lives should be about achieving that goal with dwelling with God.

Listen to God and cling to Him.

We are spiritual subcontractors tasked to build up the house of the Lord.

Make a joyful shout to the LORD, all you lands! Serve the LORD with gladness; come before His presence with singing. Know that the LORD, He is God; it is He who has made us and not we ourselves, we are His people and the sheep of His pasture. Enter into His gates with thanksgiving and into His courts with praise. Be thankful to Him and bless His name. For the LORD is good; His mercy is everlasting, and His truth endures to all generations." (Ps. 100:1–5)

You want to get to know God better? How do you get to know your new cell phone, or your new best friend? You spend time with them! Same with God!

43

Why Jesus?

Is there more to Jesus than just the name?

There are some who think they know Jesus and what He did. Let me help you out according to the Word of God, the Bible. Jesus is the Messiah that was predicted thousands of years ago, in the Old Testament. Jesus was born from a virgin. The Lord brought wise men to worship Him when He was a baby and protected Him when the evil king tried to kill Him. Yes, they murdered thousand of baby boys just to make sure Jesus was dead. It did not work.

Jesus came to show us the way God the Father wants us to live, a true and holy life. The Lord says that we are to be holy for He is holy. That is what we are to be striving for if we truly believe in Jesus. Jesus knew that his fate was to be tortured and crucified, and He did not want to go through all of the pain and suffering. Before He was arrested, He pleaded with the Father, "Please take this cup from me, but let Your will be done."

So many do not really know what He went through. Jesus was whipped "per Roman customs thirty-nine times." The whips were strands of leather with broken glass covering each strand. So every time the whip would hit Jesus, the glass would rip and tear His skin to shreds. He did this for YOU. That is not to mention the other torture He had to go through: they ripped His beard out and kicked and punched Him over and over again. He was beat up so badly He was unrecognizable.

Then they made Him carry the cross up the hill, as far as He was able, and nailed Him to it. This is what Jesus did for you and me. As I said before, He did not have to go through any of this—He chose to—for you. Through His blood that poured from His body, your sins are forgiven; and if you decide to live for Jesus to further His kingdom, you have a promise of eternal life with Him forever. He did all of this for us. We can either turn our back on Him or follow and serve Him to be used by Him to further His kingdom. We all have a choice. I choose to follow and to serve the Lord.

May the Lord bless all of you.

Jesus and only Jesus will help us to overcome the world.

When John the Baptist saw Jesus, he knew He was the Messiah sent by God.

"The next day John saw Jesus coming toward him and said, 'Behold! The Lamb of God who takes away the sin of the world!'" (John 1:29).

Only through the blood of Jesus, while hanging upon the cross, our sins are totally washed away! Thank you Jesus! Jesus freely sacrificed His life for you and for me. He promises us eternal life with Him, if we belong to Him.

He is the sacrificed lamb and He washed away our sins, if we repent of them and follow Him.

Jesus comes to give us abundant life in Him.

"For I know that my redeemer lives and He shall stand at last on the earth" (Job 19:25).

Jesus is the sum of total bliss.

"Simon Peter answered and said, 'You are the Christ, the Son of the living God'" (Matt. 16:16).

There are some people who would say: I have heard about Jesus my whole life. Yes, I believe in Him. And that is that.

There is so much more than just belief in the name of Jesus. He wants so much from you and me.

"Jesus said to him, 'I am the way, the truth, and the life. No one comes to the Father except through Me" (John 14:6).

Jesus tells us here that He is the only way to come to God the Father. He wants you to come to Him and to serve Him.

"Behold, I stand at the door and knock, if anyone hears My voice and opens the door, I will come to him" (Rev. 3:20a).

Jesus is knocking; we just have to say, "Yes, come Lord Jesus. I want you in my life; I want to live for You." He is there and waiting.

What a wonderful friend we have in Jesus. Call out to Him, and He will answer.

"In the beginning was the Word and the Word was with God and the Word was God" (John 1:1).

Jesus the Messiah is eternal. He was not just born in a manger; He always was.

"Then God said, Let Us make man in Our image, according to Our likeness" (Gen. 1:26a).

The day is coming when the Lord will wipe away every tear from our eyes. There will be no more pain; all things will become new. We are like sheep; Jesus is like our shepherd. He will never leave us and wants to be our friend forever. We just have to call upon Him.

We must have a close relationship with Jesus; we will be powerless without Him.

Jesus will give you rest from all of your dreams of worldly ambitions, but set a fire within you with a higher ambition than ever. Follow Jesus.

We can be one with God when we come to Him through Jesus.

What an undeserving privilege it is for us; as small as we are to be able to serve the Creator of all things. To be used by the Almighty God. Wow!

We need to know the Lord personally and to make Him known to others.

How well do you know your spouse and children? Do you know Jesus that well? We must constantly work on a close relationship with the Lord. He is to be your best friend. He is to be closer to you than a brother. Let Him be the one you would run to in good times and in bad. Let Him give you the comfort that is beyond all understanding. Gain a close relationship with Jesus. You will be the happiest person on earth!

Jesus says, "Truly I say unto you as you do it to the least of these, you have done it to Me" (Matt. 25:40b).

Let people see Christ in you. We all need hope. Jesus is hope. When we belong to Jesus, we have a high calling. When Jesus calls you, He calls you to die to yourself and follow Him. Greater is He that is in us than he that is in the world. Be strong and stand upon the solid rock of ages, the Lord Jesus Christ.

You can either let life knock you down or you can stand upon the solid rock of Jesus and let Him take over.

Bless Him in the morning, noon, and night. Never take your eyes off of the Lord. Try to capture His heart like King David did with constant praise and fellowship!

We are either for Jesus or against Him.

"He who is not with Me is against Me" (Matt. 12:30a).

There is no other way!

Jesus is the most influential Jew of all time.

Let us be a reflection of Jesus today. Let your friends, coworkers, and family want and hunger for what they see in you, which is Jesus.

We need the Messiah (the Lord Jesus Christ) to set us free, to transform us in our daily lives.

Have you met Him, have you been transformed? We need to be conformed and transformed in Christ not just on Sundays but everyday.

Because Jesus was dead and is now alive forever and ever, He will carry on His heavenly work of interceding for us.

"Therefore He is also able to save to the uttermost those who come to God through Him, since He always lives to make intercession for them" (Heb. 7:25).

"Who is he who condemns? It is Christ who died and furthermore is also risen, who is even at the right hand of God, who also makes intercession for us" (Rom. 8:34).

Yes, some people wonder why Jesus. Jesus makes intercession for us unto God the Father; He makes our prayers perfect before God the Father.

"For there is one God and one Mediator between God and men, the Man Christ Jesus, who gave Himself a ransom for all, to be testified in due time" (1 Tim. 2:5–6).

"The LORD your God will raise up for you a Prophet like me from your midst, from your brethren Him you shall hear,

"I will raise up for them a Prophet like you from among their brethren, and will put My words in His mouth and He shall speak to them all that I command Him" (Deut. 18:15, 18).

Jesus fulfilled this wonderful prophecy that Moses spoke about to take his place.

Jesus died for you, would you live for Him?

"And he who does not take his cross and follow after Me is not worthy of Me" (Matt. 10:38).

We need to know the Lord personally and to make Him known to others.

How are we to show Jesus to others? We show the world Jesus by letting Jesus shine through us. We need to be a reflection of Jesus with everything we say and do.

Let Jesus be the Alpha and the Omega—the beginning and the end of your trust, your love, and your witness for the Lord.

Is there anything else worth telling lost people besides Jesus Christ, and what He has done for you?

People are willing to pay a high price for something they value. Is it any surprise that Jesus would demand this much of a commitment from His followers?

When you feel like you are all alone. You are never alone; just call the name of Jesus, and He promises that He will never leave you.

We are all part of the Great Commission. We all have a job to do for the Lord.

When Jesus comes back, how do you want Him to find you? We must serve Him with all of our hearts.

Everyone knows what Easter represents. Most of the time with worldly people, it is the Easter bunny. We have to wake up!

On Easter, we shall remember the sacrificial death of our Savior Jesus the Christ. He was tortured and beat beyond recognition; and through His blood that was pouring down His body, we are saved and our sins are totally washed away.

Then on that blessed third day, our Lord rose from the grave! Thank you, Jesus, for being the sacrificial lamb on our behalf. As undeserving as we are, we are so thankful. Blessed is the Lord!

Do not ever put anybody or anything over your relationship with Jesus.

We are to be like clay, and Jesus is the potter. Let Him form and mold you to be the person He has created you to be to bring Him honor and glory through you.

Never stop falling in love with Jesus.

Who is your best friend? Who do you run to in times of trouble? Let it be Jesus, only Jesus.

Whom does your heart belong to? Let it belong to Christ.

Jesus did not die so we could keep on living for ourselves. He died so we could live for Him.

You can build a personal relationship with Jesus. Being fit to serve Him is a commitment, so prepare to take up your cross and follow Him.

Jesus is the Messiah, the Lord above all lords. He's our redeemer, our refuge, our solid rock. Stand firm upon the solid rock of the Messiah.

No one can ever love you more than Jesus. He went through great beatings and horrendous torture before being nailed to the cross, all for you.

Love so amazing; Jesus.

Who Is Jesus?

"For unto us a Child is born. Unto us a Son is given: and the government will be upon His shoulder. And His name will be called Wonderful, Counselor, Mighty God, Everlasting Father, Prince of Peace" (Isa. 9:6).

For God was pleased to have all His fullness dwell in His Son, Jesus Christ.

"For in Him dwells all the fullness of the Godhead bodily" (Col. 2:9).

"Who being the brightness of His glory and the express image of His person, and upholding all things by the word of His power, when He had by Himself purged our sins, sat down at the right hand of the Majesty on high" (Heb. 1:3).

Whenever we see the Son, we see the Father.

When we come to Christ, we come to the Father.

"As I live, says the LORD, Every knee shall bow to Me and every tongue shall confess to God" (Rom. 14:11).

He is the radiance of God's glory and the exact representation of His being.

"For God so loved the world that He gave His only begotten Son, that whoever believes in Him should not perish but have everlasting life" (John 3:16).

Whenever we see the Son, we see the Father. When we come to Christ, we come to the Father. Amen and Amen!

Jesus is a real person who lived a genuinely sinless life and died an agonizing real death on a real cross, shedding real blood for you and me. Not a philosophy, there is nothing philosophical about crucifixion!

If we leave Jesus out of our witness, we leave the sun out of the day, the moon out of the night, the waters out of the ocean. There is no gospel worth proclaiming if Jesus is left out.

News that is good ought to be spread quickly. "Go quickly and tell His disciples that He is risen from the dead" (Matt. 28:7a).

Jesus the Messiah is Lord of all. Never stop praising Him for who He is and for what He has done, is doing and will be doing.

Jesus says, "I am the good shepherd. The good shepherd gives His life for the sheep" (John 10:11).

There is no one who would ever give his or her life for you. And if someone would give their life for you, their blood will not do you any good. For only the blood of Jesus totally washes away your sins and gives you a promise of eternal life in heaven with Him. That is pretty awesome!

We should be totally thankful to the Lord Jesus Christ for everything He has done for us. We have an awesome God!

This is a faithful saying:

> For if we died with Him,
> We shall also live with Him.
> If we endure,

We shall also reign with Him.
If we deny Him,
He also will deny us. (2 Tim. 2:11–12)

Everything about Jesus revolves around love!

We should strive to be able to look deep and far, and behold the awe-inspiring glories of our risen Lord.

"Then He said to Thomas, reach your finger here, and look at My hands; and reach your hand here and put it into My side. Do not be unbelieving, but believing. And Tomas answered and said to Him, My Lord and my God!" (John 20:27–28).

Christ's resurrection proves His deity. Because He was God, it was impossible for death to keep its hold on Him.

"Whom God raised up having loosed the pains of death, because it was not possible that He should be held by it" (Acts 2:24).

The empty tomb is a sign also of our forgiveness. If Jesus had not paid the debt for our sins, He would not have risen from the grave. The empty tomb also proves that we shall rise from the dead. Christ's same body rose, so shall ours.

"A little while longer and the world will see Me no more, but you will see Me. Because I live, you will live also" (John 14:19).

44

Jesus Was Jewish

God never sent Jesus to do away with Jewishness.

If you are Jewish, then you are God's chosen people. Gentiles are grafted in through father Abraham.

We must always remember: God promised that one day He would make a new covenant with the Jewish people; the old covenant made through Moses at Mount Sinai would be transformed.

"Behold, the days are coming says the LORD, when I will make a new covenant with the house of Israel and with the house of Judah" (Jer. 31:31).

"Therefore the Lord Himself will give you a sign: Behold, the virgin shall conceive and bear a Son, and shall call His name Immanuel" (Isa. 7:14).

"For unto us a Child is born, unto us a Son is given; and the government will be upon His shoulder. And is name will be called Wonderful, Counselor, Mighty God, Everlasting Father, Prince of Peace" (Isa. 9:6).

We must never forget Isaiah 53, which describes how the Messiah will suffer and die to save the Jewish people as a nation and all people.

Yeshua came as a humble man who ultimately suffered for the sins of all humanity at the cost of His own life. He did not come as a warrior.

To understand the Bible, especially Isaiah 53, effectively is to set aside some of the ways in which we tend to prejudge the Bible; instead, allow it to speak for itself. We are to read it with an open mind and ask the Lord for full understanding.

Yeshua fulfilled the prophecies of Isaiah 53 in the first century. Other prophecies about the Messiah and His kingdom point to the high point of God's plan and focus on the events of the end of days.

Jesus was Jewish; He preached in the temple. Non-Jews were able to come in and be with them.

We are to worship the Lord Messiah with great joy!

Israel is the apple of God's eye.

The sovereign king of the Jews is the same in the Tanakh (Hebrew Bible, some call it the Old Testament) as in the B'rit Hadashah (New Testament). They are one.

The Hebrew Torah also had God speaking plural.

"Then God said, 'Let Us make man in Our image, according to Our likeness'" (Gen. 1:26a).

Jesus was the most popular Jew of all time. Blessed is the Lord Yeshua!

All of the apostles were Jewish.

If anyone is in Yeshua (Jesus), he is born again.

You hear people say, "You must be born again." Jesus said this to Nicodemus.

"Jesus answered and said to him. Most assuredly, I say to you, unless one is born again, he cannot see the kingdom of God" (John 3:3).

To be born again by a Jewish prophet! This is Jewish.

This term came from the Old Testament.

> Therefore say, thus says the Lord God: I will gather you from the peoples, assemble you from the countries where you have been scattered, and I will give you the land of Israel. And they will go there and they will take away all its detestable things and all its abominations from there. Then I will give them one heart, and I will put a new spirit within them, and take the stony heart out of their flesh and give them a heart of flesh. That they may walk in My statues and keep My judgments and do them; and they shall be My people, and I will be their God.
> But as for those whose hearts follow the desire for their detestable things and their abominations, I will recompense their deeds on their own heads, Says the Lord God. (Ezek. 11:17–21)

To stay strong in Yeshua, always remember and read Psalm 22. It tells of our Lord's death; He did it all for you. He deserves all of your love and devotion. Make sure Yeshua is number one in your life and tell as many Jews as you can why you love Him so much and why you know that He is the Messiah promised in the Tanakh.

Let Yeshua use you as His tool to populate the Lord's Kingdom with His chosen people the Jews. What a great honor!

There is not any relationship in the world more fulfilling or one that brings greater joy and peace than connection with the God of Abraham, Isaac, and Jacob. Get to know Yeshua, serve Him with all of your heart.

45

Jesus Is Coming Soon

Knowing that Christ's return will be sudden and unexpected should motivate us to be prepared. We are to live responsibly not using His tarrying as an excuse to not do God's work of being used by Him to further His kingdom.

Jesus asks us to spend our time of waiting for His return by taking care of His people and doing His work here, both in the church and outside of it. This is the best way to prepare for Christ's return.

Christ's second coming will be swift and sudden. There will be no opportunity for last-minute repentance. The choice we make will determine our destiny!

The Lord is coming very soon. How do you want Him to find you? With your hand in the cookie jar of sin, or living to serve Him?

The Lord makes it very clear that we either serve Him or Satan—there is not any in-between.

Our greatest fear should be while standing before the Lord and Him saying, "I never knew you."

We say that we believe in God, but some of us are not living like we want to go to heaven. Tomorrow may be too late.

When Jesus comes back, how do you want Him to find you? We must serve Him with all of our hearts.

"For the Son of Man will come in the glory of His Father with His angels and then He will reward each according to his works" (Matt. 16:27).

Christ's second coming will be like that of a thief—it will be totally unexpected. Therefore, it will be when due preparations for His reception has not been made. But His followers will not let that day surprise them like a thief. They will always be looking for His appearing. Never take your eyes off of the Lord. He is coming as a thief in the night; we must all be ready.

"Behold, He is coming with clouds and every eye will see Him, even they who pierced Him. And all the tribes of the earth will mourn because of Him. Even so. Amen. I am the Alpha and the Omega, the Beginning and the End. Says the Lord. Who is and who was and who is to come, the Almighty" (Rev. 1:7–8).

The Lord is coming quickly, are you going to be ready? Do you still have one foot in the world? Focus upon the Lord at all times. Be ready.

When Christ comes, we shall know whom He is and why He has come. There will no longer be any mystery or secret about the coming of the Son of Man. There will be no need to ask any questions then. No one will make a mistake about His appearing when it actually takes place. Every eye will see Him. Christ's coming will be sudden, universally visible, and as terrifying as lightning to the ungodly. Christ's coming will be the source of untold joy to His friends, but it will bring deep sorrow to His foes. All the nations of the earth will mourn because Jesus will find them unsaved. As a result, horror will be their eternal portion.

Our Lord's first concern when He returns will be the security of His elect. He has gone to prepare a place for them.

> Let not your heart be troubled; you believe in God believe also in Me. In My Father's house are many mansions. If it were not so I would have told you. I go to prepare a place for you. And if I go and prepare a place for you, I will come again and receive you to Myself; that where I am, there you may be also. (John 14:1–3)

There are a lot of people that take God for granted. Yes, we have a loving God, but we also have a jealous God. If we keep on going against His Word, disasters will hit. Remember Sodom and Gomorrah, and even Noah? Keep on reading the Word of God; Jesus tells us that disasters will hit. Our nation has to get right with our Creator, yes, our Lord is coming very soon. Are you ready?

The King is coming!

Jesus is so loving He gave His life for us. Not only that, He calls us His friends and if that were not enough, He invites us to be His bride and live with Him forever. That is the depth of His love. In return, He asks us to set our affections on things above, not on things on the earth.

"Set your mind on things above, not on things on the earth" (Col. 3:2).

He desires our love in return for His love for us.

How will the Lord find you if He would come today? Would He find you serving Him, being a wonderful reflection of Him to everyone we see? Or would He find you in the playground of the world?

He came as a lamb, but He will return as a lion!

The Lord is coming quickly, are you going to be ready? Focus upon the Lord at all times. It is so important to be ready!

> When the Son of Man comes in His glory and all the holy angels with Him then He will sit on the throne of His glory. All the nations will be gathered before Him and He will separate them one from another, as a shepherd divides his sheep from the goats. And He will set the sheep on His right hand, but the goats on the left. Then the King will say to those on His right hand, "Come, you blessed of My Father, inherit the kingdom prepared for you from the foundation of he world.
>
> Then He will also say to those on the left hand, "Depart form Me, you cursed, into the everlasting fire prepared for the devil and his angels." (Matt. 25:31–34, 41)

We must be ready for the return of Christ; we must continuously strive to "be holy for He is holy." And turn our back on the world and serve the risen Savior with all of our hearts.

46

Come to Christ

Jesus wants all of us to come to Him, to turn our backs on ourselves and to live for Him. Jesus says, "I am the way, the truth and the life. No one comes to the Father except through Me" (John 14:6).

Stop trying to live your own lives to please yourselves. Turn your back on your sinful nature and run to Jesus. He promises you eternal life in heaven with Him forever in our new bodies where "God will wipe away every tear from our eyes; there shall be no more death, nor sorrow, nor crying. There shall be no more pain for the former things have passed away" (Rev. 21:4).

We must give it up for the Lord. What you may ask? We must give up anything in our lives that we place before Him.

The Lord Jesus Christ came for you. He knows you very well. He wants you to live forever in heaven with Him. Jesus loves you more than anyone could ever love you. He gave His all for you, and He gave His life for you. And through His blood you have a great inheritance with Him forever. You just have to come to Him.

"Come to Me, all you who labor and are heavy laden, and I will give you rest. Take My yoke upon you and learn from

Me, for I am gentile and lowly in heart and you will find rest for your soul. For My yoke is easy and My burden is light" (Matt. 11:28–30).

Just like Jesus had to overcome the cross, we also have to overcome the cross that we have. The only way to overcome our cross is to keep our eyes upon Jesus; only Jesus can help us to overcome what we are going through.

"Then He said to them all. If anyone desires to come after Me, let him deny himself and take up his cross daily and follow Me" (Luke 9:23).

We must come out of the darkness and into the light of Jesus.

"Then Jesus spoke to them again, saying. I am the light of the world. He who follows Me shall not walk in darkness, but have the light of life" (John 8:12).

Jesus wants to save you from the world, and Satan is the prince of the world. Satan is darkness; he is a liar and a thief.

"The thief does not come except to steal and to kill and to destroy. I have come that they may have life and that they may have it more abundantly" (John 10:10).

Again, Jesus tells us to come out of the darkness of the world.

"I have come as a light into the world, that whoever believes in Me should not abide in darkness" (John 12:46).

47

Belief in the Lord Jesus Christ

There are some who do not yet know Jesus Christ. If you are troubled with unbelief, believe as much as you can and then cry out to the Lord.

"Immediately the father of the child cried out and said with tears, 'Lord, I believe; help my unbelief!'" (Mark 9:24).

We must also cry out: "I do believe. Help me to overcome my unbelief!"

Make sure you take down any worldly walls that you might have around you. Be teachable and ask the Lord to teach you more.

You may feel empty, like there is a hole in the center of your being. Christ is the missing piece of the puzzle of life that you have sought for so long. Satan would have you fight against this truth until you die. Turn your back on Satan, and he will flee.

Does this sound familiar?

> My God, My God, why have You forsaken Me? Why are You so far from helping Me? I'm poured out like water and all My bones are out of joint; My heart is like wax; it has melted within Me. My

strength is dried up like a potsherd and My tongue clings to My jaws; You have brought Me to the dust of death. For dogs have surrounded Me the congregation of the wicked has enclosed Me. They pierced My hands and My feet. I can count all My bones. They divide My garments among them. And for My clothing they cast lots.

No, this is not in the New Testament; it is in, Psalm 22. This is a prophecy of Jesus Christ the Messiah.

We are small, we are weak and we need His strength and wisdom. Do not turn to man, turn to Jesus!

People will leave you. Jesus never will, so run to Him.

Jesus is our example of a faithful servant. We are to learn from Him.

As small, weak, and undeserving as we are, still He gave His life for us. What an awesome God we have.

The world will neglect you and turn their back on you, but Jesus never will. Seek Him and His unconditional love. Some may say that Jesus is just another angel. According to the Scripture this is incorrect.

"Having become so much better than the angels, as He has by inheritance obtained a more excellent name than they. For to which of the angels did He ever say:

You are My Son,
Today I have begotten You?
And again:
I will be to Him a Father
And He shall be to Me a Son?

But when He again brings the firstborn into the world, He says:
Let all the angels of God worship Him.
And of the angels He says:
Who makes His angels spirits
And His ministers a flame of fire.
But to the Son He says:
Your throne O God, is forever and ever:
A scepter of righteousness is the scepter of Your kingdom.
You have loved righteousness and hated lawlessness;
Therefore God, Your God, has anointed You
With the oil of gladness more than Your companions.
And:
You, LORD in the beginning
Laid the foundation of the earth.
And the heavens are the work
Of Your hands. They will perish, but You remain:
And they will all grow old like a garment;
Like a cloak You will fold them up
And they will be changed.
But You are the same,
And Your years will not fail.
But to which of the angels has He ever said:
Sit at My right hand, till I make Your enemies Your footstool? (Heb. 1:5–13)

"The Father loves the Son and has given all things into His hand" (John 3:35).

If we believe in Jesus, He promises us eternal life with Him.

This next verse is part of a prayer that Jesus was praying to the Father:

> As You have given Him authority over all flesh,
> that He should give eternal life to as many as You
> have given Him. And this is eternal life, that they
> may know You, the only true God and Jesus Christ
> whom You have sent. (John 17:2–3)

If we really are a believer in Jesus, it is our responsibility to get righteous before the Lord and in the name of Jesus, change the world as best we can.

We must pour out all of our hope and trust into the Lord. Put Him in control and stop trying to run our own life. Give it to Jesus to run and enjoy the ride!

"Jesus said to him, 'Thomas, because you have seen Me, you have believed. Blessed are those who have not seen and yet have believed'" (John 20:29).

This verse is for you and me, even though we never saw Jesus like Thomas has; by faith we believe in Jesus. We believe that He physically rose from the dead, and we know that our Messiah is coming back very soon.

Do we want to be believers or just followers of the Lord? This is the big question.

If the world does not see any evidence that we truly believe what we claim to believe about God, why would they want it? We must all let our light of our belief in Jesus the Messiah shine, shine, shine.

We want to know Jesus. Are we willing to give up everything to know Jesus? Are you ready to let your mind be like a sponge to absorb as much of His teachings as possible? Are you consumed with serving the Lord of all creation?

Let Him be your passion. He then will shower you with blessings. He is so awesome!

To get close to the Lord, we need to know the power of His resurrection. To be conformed transformed all the time.

"Most assuredly, I say to you, he who believes in Me has everlasting life" (John 6:47).

Believe means: to have faith in, to trust and accept as true, to follow and to have complete reliance on.

"He who believes in the Son has everlasting life; and he who does not believe the Son shall not see life, but the wrath of God abides on him" (John 3:36).

"Be of good courage, and He shall strengthen your heart. All you who hope in the LORD" (Ps. 31:24).

The Bible states that the nations of the earth will mourn because unbelievers will suddenly realize they have chosen the wrong side. It will be too late for them.

48

Belong to Jesus

Do we belong to Christ? This is the most important question that you can ask yourself. Do people see Christ in you, or do they see worldliness, which is sinfulness? Do we live our lives as a representative of Jesus? Do we live our lives according to what society says is okay, or according to the way the Scriptures tells us to live our lives?

Do we say, "Oh, we do not have to get married. People do not do that anymore, let's just live together"? That is Satan's lie to draw you away from God! Yes, the Bible never changes—it was the same yesterday, today, and forever. Society changes, and in the process, draws people away from our Creator, away from our God. "For the wages of sin is death, but the gift of God is eternal life in Christ Jesus our Lord" (Rom. 6:23). Death is eternal separation from God. How sad.

If we belong to the Lord, our lives are no longer our own. We must trust in Him with all of our hearts. We tend to lean on our own understanding instead of trusting God with all our hearts. We have to let go of trying to lead our own lives. Wherever God sends us, He will guard our lives. We belong to Him.

Remember, if you really belong to Jesus: His best friends were His apostles, not worldly friends. One bad apple can lead you astray.

"He who has seen Me has seen the Father" (John 14:9b).

If you want to know God, you must know the Son! You must be focused on eternity; stay focused only on heavenly things.

"And this is eternal life, that they may know You the only true God and Jesus Christ whom You have sent" (John 17:3).

Ask the Holy Spirit to help you gain a close personal relationship with the Lord Jesus Christ. Have faith, He will.

We must take our eyes off of the world and its sinfulness, focus upon being the person God created us to be. We must strive to be close to Him and to serve Him.

We belong to Jesus. We are His ambassadors. Let us make Him proud of us today! How awesome to be used by the Lord to further His Kingdom!

When we serve other people and share the Lord with them, we are not only doing it to help the Lord's children, we are doing it unto the Lord!

"Assuredly, I say to you, inasmuch as you did it to one of the least of these My brethren, you did it to Me" (Matt. 25:40b).

We must not be idle; if we belong to Jesus, we must serve Him. We must be His ambassadors, His reflection wherever we go. This is what it means to belong to Christ.

But as it is written: "Eye has not seen, nor ear heard, nor have entered into the heart of man the things which God has prepared for those who love Him" (1 Cor. 2:9).

"Therefore, if anyone is in Christ, he is a new creation; old things have passed away; behold all things have become new" (2 Cor. 5:17).

Are you different? Are you a new person in Christ Jesus? If you belong to Jesus you must strive to be that new person. Take a look at your past. Are you totally different? Do people see a change in you for the better? Do they see Christ in you?

"For whoever does the will of My Father in heaven is My brother and sister and mother" (Matt. 12:50).

Take a step back and look at your life. Are you doing your will or the will of the Lord? Be very careful, doing the will of the Lord is "not living in the world but living for the kingdom of the Lord." Does Jesus consider you His brother, sister, mother?

The more understanding that the Lord will give you, that much more will be demanded of you.

We are not to keep Jesus to ourselves; we must serve Him with what He has given us. We must simply know the Lord. We must surrender to the Lord.

I love the book of Psalm. It is good to read and follow the examples of the writers.

Just like King David tried to capture the heart of God, we also are to follow his teachings; we also are to try to capture the heart of God with our praise, worship, and service for Him.

"In God we boast all day long and praise Your name forever" (Ps. 44:8).

Never stop boasting about the Lord! He is our strength and our life is in Him.

If we belong to Jesus, we have to be a new person in Christ Jesus. The Lord will not honor someone who clings to sin and the world. We must be 100 percent changed and turn our back on our past worldly lives. We are to live for Him, and He promises us eternal life with Him.

To belong to Jesus, we must be changed from the inside out. We must bear good fruit for all to see. We are His ambassadors. Like Paul, we have a race to run for our Lord! The prize at the finish line is eternal! Do not let Satan sidetrack you!

Let Jesus be proud of us in the way we live our lives serving Him. Turning our back on self and focusing on being His ambassadors. Never take your eyes off of the risen Lord! Let Him lead and guide you everyday.

Jesus said that the world would hate you. It is okay, let them. We belong to Jesus.

We are in Christ, and Christ is in us. What a wonderful combination of the Father, Christ, and us! Praise the Lord!

We are to set our eyes on things above, not on things of the earth.

We must be crucified with Christ; we are to present our lives as a living sacrifice to Him.

"I beseech you therefore brethren, by the mercies of God, that you present your bodies a living sacrifice, holy acceptable to God which is your reasonable service. And do not be conformed to this world, but be transformed by the renewing of your mind. That you may prove what is that good and acceptable and perfect will of God" (Rom. 12:1–2).

Jesus must become greater in our lives, while we become less.

49

Holy Spirit

"Do you not know that you are the temple of God and that the Spirit of God dwells in you? If anyone defiles the temple of God, God will destroy him. For the temple of God is holy, which temple you are" (1 Cor. 3:16–17).

The Holy Spirit will help us to live our lives pleasing to the Lord. Be careful not to pollute the temple of the Lord with alcohol or drugs—how horrible that would be! Always remember we are His temple; do not defile it. With the person who does, it stands to question if he really belong to the Lord?

"But you are not in the flesh but in the Spirit, if indeed the Spirit of God dwells in you. Now if anyone does not have the Spirit of Christ, he is not His" (Rom. 8:9).

Paul is telling us that if we belong to Christ, then the Holy Spirit of God dwells in us. How awesome is that! Our bodies are the temple of God's Holy Spirit. So then, we are not to pollute our bodies with anything unclean or worldly.

"There is therefore now no condemnation to those who are in Christ Jesus. Who do not walk according to the flesh, but according to the Spirit" (Rom. 8:1).

Lean on the Holy Spirit to give you understanding; let Him help you in your walk with the Lord.

Our lives are not to be controlled by our evil impulses. We need a relationship with the Lord everyday. The only way is to submit to the Spirit of God.

Remember that God has not given us a spirit of fear, but of power, of love, and of a sound mind. So do not be ashamed of the testimony of our Lord Jesus Christ.

Christians do not simply believe in Christ or imitate Christ from a distance. We have been united to Jesus Christ by the power of the Spirit.

"For those who live according to the flesh, set their minds on the things of the flesh. But those who live according to the Spirit, the things of the Spirit. For to be carnally minded is death, but to be spiritually minded is life and peace" (Rom. 5–6).

Without a close relationship with the Holy Spirit, you will be tossed around like the wind in the waves. He is our helper.

Listen to the Holy Spirit when He would put you into such a frame of mind, that you should at once yield to the divine instruction, which says, "Believe in the Lord Jesus Christ, and thou shalt be saved."

If you live for the Lord, remember: He that is in you (which is the Holy Spirit) is greater than he who is in the world.

To belong to Jesus, we must walk in the Spirit of the Lord, and we shall not fulfill the lust of the flesh.

Those who are Christ's have crucified the flesh with its passions and desires. If we live in the spirit, let us also walk in the Spirit.

We cannot save ourselves; the Lord will save us. We need the new Spirit, without the new Spirit, we cannot please God.

A man does not win souls to Christ while he is himself half asleep. We must be wide-awake and quickened by the Spirit of God.

"For the Holy Spirit will teach you in that very hour what you ought to say" (Luke 12:12).

We need the Holy Spirit of the Lord to set us free, to transform us in our daily lives.

The only way to please the Lord is to submit to the Spirit of God. Let Him lead you to the Lord.

We as followers of Christ are to be filled with the Spirit, walk in the Spirit of God.

"The eyes of the Lord are on the righteous and His ears are open to their cry" (Ps. 34:15).

Christians do not simply believe in Christ or imitate Christ from a distance. We have been united to Jesus Christ by the power of the Spirit.

Let the Holy Spirit be your pilot in leading your life and you are the copilot. Let go of the steering wheel in faith and let Him take over.

"If we belong to Jesus, then our bodies are the temple of the Holy Spirit of God. "Do you not know that your body is a temple of the Holy Spirit, who is in you, whom you have received from God? You are not your own; you were bought at a price. Therefore honor God with your body" (1 Cor. 6:19–20).

We are to take the Word of God very seriously. Be very careful not to defile your body, the Lord's temple, with sin, sex, and drugs. We must be a reflection of Christ.

Lean on the Holy Spirit to give you understanding, let Him help you in your walk with the Lord.

Just as David would seek the face of the Lord, we are to follow his lead. With the Holy Spirit's help, seek the face of Jesus. Praise and bless the Lord.

"However, when He the Spirit of truth, has come. He will guide you into all truth; for He will not speak on His own authority, but whatever He hears He will speak and He will tell you things to come" (John 16:13).

Your deeds will not save you; the Lord will clean us and give us a new heart, a new spirit. We must repent and turn from our worldliness and live for Christ.

50

Holy

"Holy, holy, holy Lord God Almighty, who was and is and is to come!" (Rev. 4:8b).

Continuous worship of the Lord is what is going on in heaven right now.

"God reigns over the nations; God sits on His holy throne" (Ps. 47:8).

If we belong to the Lord, we must have and display Holy standards.

Holiness has been given to us as a gift.

"For I am the LORD your God. You shall therefore consecrate yourselves and you shall be holy for I am holy" (Lev. 11:44).

We are to never stop striving to be holy for the Lord. Jesus was set apart for a holy purpose we have been called; we have been set apart to become God's holy people. We all have been given the keys to eternal life.

Our standards should be much higher than the rest of the worlds. We have a higher calling; we must pick up our cross daily.

We need to die to ourselves, to give up our own lives and to follow the Lord.

It is so sad when Christians accept and tolerate unholy alliances. This is not glorifying the Lord. Holiness is not a concept; it is your Father's commandment for how you must live before Him.

We have to make godly decisions, and the only way we can is through the writings in the Bible. We are to live what we read.

We need to remove unholy alliances in our lives if we are to have an appetite for truth.

51

Worship

When the Lord blesses you, give it back to Him. Yes, we are not to keep the blessings that the Lord gives to us. We must bless others or give it back to Him in worship. During the worship service at church, do not just read and sing the words. Worship the Lord with all of your heart, bless Him with your worship, bless Him with the blessings He has given to you.

"Be exalted, O God above the heavens; Let Your glory be above all the earth" (Ps. 57:5).

A big question is: how do you worship during the worship service at church? Do you sing praises to the worship team? Sing the praises to the air? Are you without any emotion and just go through the motions? Do any of these really give praise and glory to the Lord? True worship is to worship the Lord with all of your heart, soul and strength. Do not worship the service leaders. I urge you to memorize the songs and to close your eyes, picture the face of Jesus and sing your worship to Him with everything you have. Try to capture the heart of Jesus with your worship.

Praise Him! Jesus our blessed Redeemer! Who freely gave His life for you and for me! Through His blood our sins are totally washed away.

"I will praise the LORD according to His righteousness and will sing praise to the name of the LORD Most High" (Ps. 7:17).

In good times and in bad times, never stop praising the Lord. The moment you do stop, you start falling into a pit of depression.

"O LORD, our Lord, how excellent is Your name in all the earth. Who have set Your glory above the heavens!"(Ps. 8:1).

All day and night there is "praise" going on in heaven. The Lord wants us also to always be in constant contact with Him, to keep on praising Him! Never take your eyes off of the Lord.

"I will praise You, O LORD, with my whole heart; I will tell of all Your marvelous works. I will be glad and rejoice in You; I will sing praise to Your name, O Most High" (Ps. 9:1–2).

Yes! We are to learn from King David and praise the Lord with all of our hearts.

Bless Him in the morning, noon and at night. Never take your eyes off of the Lord, try to capture His heart like King David did with constant praise!

> My heart is steadfast, O God, my heart is steadfast; I will sing and give praise. Awake, my glory! Awake, lute and harp! I will awaken he dawn. I will praise You, O Lord, among the peoples; I will sing to You among the nations. For Your mercy reaches unto the heavens and Your truth unto the clouds. Be exalted,

O God, above the heavens; Let Your glory be above
all the earth. (Ps. 57:7–11)

We have an awesome God! Worship Him and praise His
holy name, not only today but every day. Great is the Lord
and so worthy of all our praise!

Give your life to the Lord and bless Him, for He is
so worthy.

"O God, You are my God; early will I seek You" (Ps. 63:1a).

Seek Him with all of your heart.

"Be exalted O God, above the heavens; Let Your glory be
above all the earth" (Ps. 57:5).

"Your mercy reaches unto the heavens and Your truth unto
the clouds" (Ps. 57:10).

We silence the enemy (Satan) when we praise the Lord.
Let everything that has breath, Praise the Lord!

When you go to church to worship and have only pretended
to adore Christ, you have mocked Him by an insincere
worship and put the purple robe on Him once again. That
purple robe meant they made Him a king in name only, and
the honor that they paid Him was just a show of mockery.
Do not let this be you. Worship the Lord with all of your
heart, mind, and soul. Seek the face of Jesus and worship
Him with everything you have.

Great is the Lord and so worthy of our daily praise!

We have an awesome God! Worship Him and praise His
holy name, not only today but everyday.

Why do we praise Him? He is worthy of our praises. When going through good times, praise Him. When we are suffering never stop giving Him praise. He is worthy of our praises; He is so worthy.

Rejoice in the Lord always! Again I say rejoice!

- If we do not praise the Lord, the rocks will shout out in praise!

- Praise Him when you are upset and depressed! You will get the victory!

- The victory is won through praise and worship of the Lord!

- We silence the enemy when we praise the Lord.

- The enemy flees when we call upon the name of Jesus. Worship Him; praise Him!

- The battle is not yours; the battle belongs to the Lord! Praise Him!

- Shower the Lord with praise in the morning, afternoon and at night. Never stop giving Him praise. He is so worthy.

- Be exalted, O God, above the heavens; let Your glory be above all the earth. Your mercy reaches unto the heavens and Your truth unto the clouds.

- Jesus the Messiah is worthy of all our praise and worship!

- Stand up in the darkness for the King of Kings and the Lord of Lords

- The King is on the throne! Let everything that has breath, praise the Lord!

Praise Him with all of your heart, soul, and strength. Praise the one who was, is and is to come.

He is the King of kings and the Lord of lords! Praise Him!

"O come, let us worship and bow down; let us kneel before the LORD our Maker. For He is our God, and we are the people of His pasture and the sheep of His hand" (Ps. 95:6–7a).

Praise Him during extreme happiness as well as great trials. Never stop praising Him.

In heaven, there is constant worship going on. The Lord created us to also give Him constant worship. Give Him praise always throughout the day and night.

Before we begin to give praise and worship to our Lord, we must prepare ourselves. Pray for the Holy Spirit to help you to focus only upon Him and to praise Him with all of your heart. When we come into the Holy of Holies; we are to enter with thanksgiving and humble ourselves. Then we praise the Lord and worship Him.

We were made to have fellowship with the Lord and to worship Him.

We are to worship the Lord with all of our heart, soul and strength.

"To You O Lord, I lift up my soul" (Ps. 25:1).

King David was always trying to capture the heart of God. We are not any different. We should also offer up to the Lord everything we have, in worship.

52

Kingdom of God

The kingdom of God is such a mystery that our old nature cannot see or understand it. We must bury our worldly eyes and just look out of our "spiritual eyes." As Jesus says, we must be born again. We must bury our old nature and be new people in Christ Jesus. There must be a radical change in you, a new birth from heaven. If you have the new birth, you will see "the kingdom of God.

What an awesome God we have. He wants us to serve Him, to be used as His ambassadors to expand His Kingdom. We can continue to live our lives in the sinful world, or we can make a U-turn in our life and serve the Almighty God. We all have a choice.

The kingdom of God is about growth; we must grow in the Lord and cling to Him.

"Then the King will say to those on His right hand. Come, you blessed of My Father, inherit the kingdom prepared for you from the foundation of the world" (Matt. 25:34).

Do you live your life to hear these words from the Lord?

"Jesus answered, most assuredly, I say to you, unless one is born of water and the Spirit, he cannot enter the kingdom of God" (John 3:5).

We must live our lives, not for ourselves, but for the kingdom. Give it all for Jesus, just as He gave His all for us.

"Your kingdom is an everlasting kingdom and Your dominion endures throughout all generations" (Ps. 145:13).

Jesus tells us not to look back (on your worldly life)., just keep your eyes looking forward. If you keep looking back to your past you will be drawn back you will not be fit for the kingdom. Keep on striving for a hunger to search for that close relationship with the Lord, to strive to be used by Him to further His kingdom.

53

Spirituality

Spirituality is a growth towards wholeness.

We need to embrace spiritual wholeness; we need to go and get it. We need to embrace the healing that is available to us. It will not just come to us; we must go and get it.

If your mind is always on worldly things, then your mind is not on the things of the Spirit. You will not grow spiritually. Change your mind-set on what you are focusing on. Keep your eyes upon the Lord at all times, and you will grow spiritually.

We need to take a step of obedience to be healed. Embrace wholeness spiritually.

We all have been given spiritual gifts to use. If you do not know what your gift is, then just ask Jesus, He will tell you.

"Brethren, if a man is overtaken in any trespass, you who are spiritual restore such a one in a spirit of gentleness, considering yourself lest you also be tempted" (Gal. 6:1).

Paul is referring to people who are spiritual, who continue to live and walk by the Spirit to help and restore the one who has gone astray. That would be you and I. We must stay spiritually-minded and ready to help anyone who is having a hard time spiritually.

Spiritual health depends on daily worship of the Lord and prayer. We can have victory through the Lord.

Call upon Jesus and tell Him that you want to know Him, that you want a close relationship with Him. Call upon Him, and He will come to you!

Remember, you are whom you hang around with. Do not hang around with the unsaved. They can bring you spiritually down and away from the Lord.

We must get serious about our spiritual life now, or we might not make it.

54

Death

There are so many people living for the "here and now." They are in their own little world, enjoying life comfortably, but ignoring the fact that their death is not only inevitable but much nearer than they think.

To have knowledge of what happens after death will be of great joy. So many people will say that they are afraid to die. If you know Scripture, it will be a joyous occasion. To be prepared to die is to be prepared to live; to be ready for eternity is what our life should be about. Look for Jesus, and He will find you. Love Him and serve Him. You will then be prepared for death.

To be unprepared for death and to know that it may come at any moment is a good reason to be afraid.

The Lord will not accept us on our terms; it will be on the Lord's terms.

"And as it is appointed for men to die once, but after this the judgment" (Heb. 9:27).

Do not think that since your spouse is living for the Lord that you can hang onto their apron strings and get in on their pass. No. This is not the way it works. If you think that you will get to heaven just because you have a loved one there, you are deceiving yourself. It is an individual matter; you have to be proven unto the Lord by how you lived your life, and He will be the judge to receive you or to turn you away. Please be careful with everything you do and say. Do it unto the Lord.

"We are confident, yes, well pleased rather to be absent from the body and to be present with the Lord" (2 Cor. 5:8).

"For I am hard-pressed between the two, having a desire to depart and be with Christ, which is far better" (Phil. 1:23).

The empty tomb proves that we also shall rise from the dead. Christ's same body rose, so shall ours. "Because I live you also shall live."

For the Lord Himself will descend from heaven with a shout, with the voice of an archangel and with the trumpet of God. And the dead in Christ will rise first. Then we who are alive and remain shall be caught up together with them in the clouds to meet the Lord in the air. And thus we shall always be with the Lord" (1 Thess. 4:16–17).

Yes! Where Jesus is now, this is where we are going to be. Be encouraged!

We must keep our eyes focused only upon the Lord.

Jesus encourages us with the following:

"A little while longer and the world will see Me no more, but you will see Me. Because I live, you will live also" (John 14:19).

This verse is great encouragement; Jesus is telling us that even as our earthly bodies will die, we will live with Him forever.

In the book of Psalms, we are encouraged about death:

"For this is God, our God forever and ever; He will be our guide even to death" (Ps. 48:14).

"You will guide me with Your counsel and afterward receive me to glory" (Ps. 73:24).

"Precious in the sight of the LORD is the death of His saints" (Ps. 116:15).

There are some who are afraid of death. "Yea, though I walk through the valley of the shadow of death. I will fear no evil; for You are with me; Your rod and Your staff, they comfort me" (Ps. 23:4).

We are not to fear death; the Lord will lead and guide us through our journey.

55

Judgment

The Lord tells us that those who hear the gospel but do not live it, on the day of judgment, He will say:

"Many will say to Me in that day, 'Lord, Lord, have we not prophesied in Your name, cast out demons in Your name and done many wonders in Your name? And then I will declare to them, I never knew you; depart from Me you who practice lawlessness!'" (Matt. 7:22–23).

Each of us shall give account of himself to God. So please live a pure righteous life.

"For we must all appear before the judgment seat of Christ, that each one may receive the things done in the body, according to what he has done, whether good or bad" (2 Cor. 5:10).

We do not just show up before the great judge of all the earth, we are not to treat Him as common. He is the great Creator. We are to prepare every day throughout our lives here on earth for that day.

There will be a time when God the Father will say "That is enough!" Like Sodom and Gomorrah, He will not tolerate man's sin anymore. He will say: "That is enough!"

God's wrath is nothing to play around with. Turn your back on sin while there is still time. Waiting may be too late.

56

Heaven

Oh, to be in heaven with the Lord should be the believer's only thought. We shall be forever with the Lord and nothing more or better can be imagined.

"Whom have I in heaven but You? And there is none upon earth that I desire besides You. My flesh and my heart fail; but God is the strength of my heart and my portion forever" (Ps. 73:25–26).

All Christians should be heavenly minded, keeping our eyes off worldliness and constantly upon heaven, upon Jesus. He will help us to overcome the world!

"Therefore whoever humbles himself as this little child is the greatest in the kingdom of heaven" (Matt. 18:4).

There is a book in heaven with the name of everyone who lives for the Lord. The Lord tells us in the next couple of verses about the book.

"He who overcomes shall be clothed in white garments, and I will not blot out his name from the Book of Life; but I will confess his name before My Father and before His angels" (Rev. 3:5).

This next verse is in reference to the New Jerusalem, where we will be living with the Lord.

"But there shall by no means enter it anything that defiles, or causes an abomination or a lie, but only those who are written in the Lamb's Book of Life" (Rev. 21:27).

Only the people whose names are written in the Lamb's Book of Life will be in the New Jerusalem. Live your life for Christ, and your name will be there.

We are to keep our eyes on heaven, upon Jesus, and He will carry us through every situation, through our life here on earth.

As Christians, we are to be heavenly minded, keeping our eyes off of worldliness and constantly upon heaven, upon Jesus.

People are so concerned about pleasing others that they end up neglecting Jesus. People pleasing will not get you into Heaven.

Our home is in heaven; we are just traveling through this world.

We could never climb our way up to heaven, so God reached down to earth. He came to us on the day we celebrate Christmas.

> Let not your heart be troubled; you believe in God, believe also in Me. In My Father's house are many mansions; if it were not so, I would have told you. I go to prepare a place for you. And if I go and prepare a place for you, I will come again and receive you

to Myself; that where I am, there you may be also.
(John 14:1–3)

This verse is so encouraging. The Lord tells us that there is a
home being build for us in heaven and when it is complete
He will bring us home to be with Him.

> "For our citizenship is in heaven, from which we also
> eagerly wait for the Savior, the Lord Jesus Christ,
> who will transform our lowly body that it may
> be conformed to His glorious body" (Philippians
> 3:20–21a).

I love this verse also. We will have brand new bodies, and
He will transform our weak bodies to be conformed to be
like the body of our Lord's.

What is going on in heaven now? Scripture tells us in the
book of Revelation. John was brought spiritually up to
heaven, and he writes what he saw.

> After these things I looked and behold a door
> standing open in heaven and the first voice which
> I heard was like a trumpet speaking with me saying
> come up here, and I will show you things which
> must take place after this. And immediately I was
> in the Spirit; and behold a throne set in heaven and
> One sat on the throne and He who sat there was like
> jasper and a sardius stone in appearance; and there
> was a rainbow around the throne, in appearance like
> an emerald. Around the throne were twenty-four
> elders sitting, clothed in white robes; and they had
> crowns of gold on their heads. And from the throne
> preceded lightnings, thunderings, and voices. Seven
> lamps of fire were burning before the throne, which

are the seven Spirits of God. Before the throne there was a sea of glass like crystal. And in the midst of the throne, and around the throne were four living creatures full of eyes in front and in back. The first living creature was like a lion, the second living creature like a calf, the third living creature had a face like a man in the fourth living creature was like a flying eagle. The four living creatures, each having six wings, were full of eyes around and within. And they do not rest day or night saying:

Holy, holy, holy, Lord God Almighty, who was and is and is to come!" (Rev. 4:1–8)

And I heard a loud voice from heaven saying. "Behold, the tabernacle of God is with men and He will dwell with them and they shall be His people. God Himself will be with them and be their God." And God will wipe away every tear from their eyes; there shall be no more death, nor sorrow, nor crying. There shall be no more pain, for the former things have passed away. Then He who sat on the throne said, "Behold, I make all things new." And He said to me, "Write, for these words are true and faithful." And He said to me, "It is done! I am the Alpha and the Omega, the Beginning and the End. I will give of the fountain of the water of life freely to him who thirsts. He who overcomes shall inherit all things. And I will be his God and he shall be My son. (Rev. 21:3–7)

57

Eternity

Be very careful how you live your life, how you spend eternity is up to you.

Life is not about the here and now—it is about eternity.

The Lord has a great promise for you of eternal life with Him. You just have to change and stop giving Satan all the glory in your life.

If we let success go to our head, someday failure will break our heart. Only success in our Lord really counts for it will last throughout eternity.

Seek eternal life with Jesus with all your heart; never take your eyes off of Him.

Jesus does not want part of us; He wants all of us. Give your life to Him. He gave His for you, and He promises you eternal life forever with Him.

Let us get into fellowship with Christ, give ourselves to Him without reserve and see life in an eternal light, looking ahead to the reward. We must have obedience in our faith to keep our eyes upon the Lord at all times and just have Him lead us.

Like Paul, we have a race to run for our Lord. The prize at the finish line is eternal! Do not let Satan sidetrack you!

Draw your attention to the distinction between the things that are seen (which are not your portion) and the things which are not seen (which are your true heritage).

Are you able to say as Paul says? "For me, to live is Christ and to die is gain."

What does he mean? To live his life for the glory of Jesus and when he dies he will have eternal life with the Lord. Yes!

This world is temporary; we are to live for eternity. As Jesus promises, if we serve Him, we will be where He is forever.

It is good for our thoughts to be: my home is in heaven; I'm just traveling through this world.

If you are not glorifying the Lord with everything you say and do, then you are not living for the Lord, and your inheritance is eternal separation from God. How horrible!

"For the wages of sin is death, but the gift of God is eternal life in Christ Jesus our Lord" (Rom. 6:23).

In Scripture, death is eternal separation from God.

Live your life glorifying the Lord with everything you do and your inheritance is eternal life with Jesus Christ the Lord.

"Whoever drinks of this water will thirst again, but whoever drinks of the water that I shall give him will never thirst. But the water that I shall give him will become in him a fountain of water springing up into everlasting life" (John 4:13–14).

Our spiritual water is the Word of God; we must read it, learn it, and live it. We will then have eternal life through Jesus Christ our Lord.

This world is temporary; we are to live for eternity. As Jesus promises, if we serve Him we will be where He is forever.

It is not easy serving the Lord. We have to stay strong, and the reward is eternal!

Pursue righteousness, godliness, faith, love, patience, and gentleness. Fight the good fight of faith and lay hold on eternal life through Jesus Christ our Lord.

"And as Moses lifted up the serpent in the wilderness, even so must the Son of Man be lifted up. That whoever believes in Him should not perish but have eternal life. For God so loved the world that He gave His only begotten Son, that whoever believes in Him should not perish but have everlasting life" (John 3:14–16).

Let us look at the words *believes in, believe, believer*:

- to be devoted to;
- being a disciple;
- a follower;
- a supporter;
- to have trust in;
- have confidence in;
- to have faith in;

- to cling to.

This is what it means to believe in Jesus Christ.

"Not that anyone has seen the Father, except He who is from God; He has seen the Father. Most assuredly, I say to you, he who believes in Me has everlasting life" (John 6:46–47).

"Most assuredly, I say to you, he who hears My Word and believes in Him who sent Me has everlasting life and shall not come into judgment, but has passed from death into life" (John 5:24).

Yes, the Lord is stating here that when our heart stops beating, our spirit that never dies will live forever.

"I am the resurrection and the life. He who believes in Me, though he may die, he shall live" (John 11:25).

I love the Word of God; it is filled with so much encouragement!

We are like sheep, and Jesus is our shepherd. We are to follow Him.

"My sheep hear My voice and I know them and they follow Me and I give them eternal life and they shall never perish; neither shall anyone snatch them out of My hand. My Father who has given them to Me, is greater than all; and no one is able to snatch them out of My Father's hand. I and My Father are one" (John 10:27–30).

If we belong to Jesus, we are His sheep and He is our shepherd. We are to follow Him and serve Him. We belong to the Lord Jesus Christ.

"He who loves his life will lose it and he who hates his life in this world will keep it for eternal life" (John 12:25).

This world is temporary; we are to live for eternity with our God.

"He who believes in the Son has everlasting life; and he who does not believe the Son shall not see life, but the wrath of God abides on him" (John 3:36).

"That whoever believes in Him should not perish but have eternal life. For God so loved the world that he gave His only begotten Son, that whoever believes in Him should not perish but have everlasting life" (John 3:15–16).

> And behold, a certain lawyer stood up and tested Him, saying. Teacher, what shall I do to inherit eternal life? He said to him. What is written in the law? What is our reading of it? So He answered and said. You shall love the LORD your God with all your heart, with all your soul, with all your strength and with all your mind. And your neighbor as yourself. (Luke 10:25–27)

"My sheep hear My voice and I know them and they follow Me and I give them eternal life and they shall never perish; neither shall anyone snatch them out of My hand" (John 10:27–28).

58

Inheritance

"And whatever you do, do it heartily as to the Lord and not to men. Knowing that from the Lord you will receive the reward of the inheritance; for you serve the Lord Christ" (Col. 3:23–24).

This is for you and for me. If we serve the Lord Jesus Christ, He has promised us a great inheritance. Be careful not to live for self, but in all we do, do it to glorify the Lord. We all have a race to run in our life here, and Jesus is at the finish line. Let Him be proud of us in the way we lived our lives by serving Him, turning our back on self, and focusing on being His ambassadors.

"The LORD knows the days of the upright. And their inheritance shall be forever" (Ps. 37:18).

Yes, He knows the number of days we have here on earth. If we live for Him, He promises us an inheritance with Him forever. This is so encouraging!

"O LORD, You are the portion of my inheritance and my cup; You maintain my lot. The lines have fallen to me in pleasant places; Yes, I have a good inheritance" (Ps. 16:5–6).

If you are not glorifying the Lord with everything you say and do, then you are not living for the Lord and your inheritance is eternal separation from God. How horrible.

Live your life glorifying the Lord with everything you do and your inheritance is eternal life with Jesus Christ the Lord.

Whatever you do, do it heartily as to the Lord and not to men. Knowing that from the Lord, you will receive the reward of the inheritance for you serve the Lord Jesus Christ.

"For You, O God have heard my vows; You have given me the heritage of those who fear Your name" (Ps. 61:5).

If we serve the Lord, He has promised us a great inheritance. Be careful not to live for self, but in all we do, do it to glorify the Lord.

"For the LORD loves justice and does not forsake His saints; they are preserved forever" (Ps. 37:28a).

(In Paul's writings, the word *saint* means followers, servants of the Lord.)

The Lord's people will be living in the New Jerusalem (our inheritance forever). Nothing impure will ever enter it, nor will anyone who does what is shameful or deceitful.

> The twelve gates were twelve pearls: Each individual gate was of one pearl and the street of the city was pure gold, like transparent glass. But I saw no temple in it, for the Lord God Almighty and the Lamb are its temple. The city had no need of the sun or of the

moon to shine in it, for the glory of God illuminated it. The Lamb is its light. And the nations of those who are saved shall walk in it's light and the kings of the earth bring their glory and honor into it. Its gates shall not be shut at all by day (there shall be no night there). And they shall bring the glory and the honor of the nations into it. But there shall by no means enter it anything that defiles, or causes an abomination or a lie, but only those who are written in the Lamb's Book of Life." (Rev. 21:21–27)

For more deeper encouragement, I highly recommend my first book, *Encouragement*. You will be blessed.